DISEASES

2nd Revised Edition

Volume 8

Spider bites to Zoonoses

Bryan Bunch

EDITOR
SCIENTIFIC PUBLISHING

GROLIER
EDUCATIONAL

Editor: Bryan Bunch

Design and production: G & H SOHO, Inc.
 Design: Gerry Burstein
 Prepress: Kathie Kounouklos

Writers: **Illustrators:**

Barbara Branca   *Editorial assistant:*   *Photographs:*
Bryan Bunch   Marianne Bunch   Karin L. Rhines
Barbara A. Darga
Betsy Feist   *Copyediting and index:*   *Icons:*
Gene R. Hawes   Felice Levy   Steve Virkus and Karen Presser
Wendy B. Murphy
Karin L. Rhines   *Creative assistance:*   *Medical Illustrations:*
Jenny Tesar   Pam Forde   Jean Cassels
Bruce Wetterau   Leslie Dunlap
Gray Williams   Pamela Johnson
                                                       Joel Snyder

Library of Congress Cataloging in Publication Data

Main entry under title:
Diseases
v. < >' cm
Includes bibliographical references and index.
Summary: Alphabetically arranged articles present medical information
on more than 500 diseases, discussing causes, symptoms, stages of the
disease, its likelihood of striking, treatments, prevention, and long-term effects.

Set ISBN: 0-7172-5688-X
1. Diseases—Encyclopedias, Juvenile. [1. Diseases—
Encyclopedias.] I. Grolier Educational Corporation
R130.5 D57 1996
616.003—dc20

96-27606
CIP
AC

Revised edition published 2003.
First published in the United States in 1997 by
Grolier Educational, Sherman Turnpike, Danbury, CT 06816

COPYRIGHT © 2003, 1997 by SCIENTIFIC PUBLISHING, INC.

A HUDSON GROUP BOOK

Set ISBN: 0-7172-5688-X

Volume ISBN: 0-7172-5696-0

Spider bites

INJURY

Emergency Room

Only two kinds of poisonous spider native to the United States pose a potential danger to people—the *black widow* and the *tarantula*. But an import from South America, the *brown recluse*, has for some years been a danger in the South and along the East Coast. Recently, a European import that is thriving in the Pacific Northwest, the *hobo spider* (*Tegenaria agrestis*), has caused severe illness and at least one death from its bite. Many other species of spiders are poisonous, but their fangs are not able to break through a person's skin to inject the toxin.

Descriptions: Only the female of the black widow species is considered dangerous. About an inch long, she is much larger than the male and has a black body with a characteristic red hourglass marking on her belly. (Sometimes the marking will show as spots or triangles.) Black widows are more common in warmer regions of the United States but can be found throughout the country. They especially like dark, damp places.

The brown recluse spider grows to about half an inch long, and its back is emblazoned with a violin-shaped mark. Its venom is potent but does most of its damage in the immediate area of the bite.

Tarantulas are large, hairy wolf spiders that can grow to two inches in body length and five inches overall, including their legs. They are found throughout the Southwest. Tarantulas look frightening but are not very dangerous because their venom is very mild. They rarely bite unless provoked. When irritated they may instead rub special hairs off their bellies and throw them with their hind legs. The hairs can cause a skin rash, though not all people are sensitive to them.

The hobo spider resembles the brown recluse—moderately large with long legs, brown with gray markings. Hobo spiders build funnel-shaped webs in or near the lower reaches of homes; they are mostly found in basements, crawl spaces, and nearby woodpiles.

If you think you have been bitten by any of the four poisonous spiders, get medical attention as soon as possible, especially if you have an immediate bad reaction to the bite.

Cause: Black widow venom is a neurotoxin that causes a spreading paralysis, usually beginning with thigh, back, and

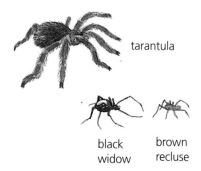

tarantula

black widow   brown recluse

The three poisonous spiders most commonly encountered in the United States are the very large tarantula, the somewhat large black widow, and the moderately sized brown recluse. The hobo spider (not shown here) is about the same size and color as the brown recluse, with which it is sometimes confused.

Phone doctor

Tetanus shot

shoulder muscles. Venom from the female brown recluse is more potent than from the male, but in either case the poison does most of its damage by destroying tissue. The effect of a hobo bite is similar to that of a brown recluse, although it can lead to severe anemia as well. Tarantula venom is very mild and rarely causes anything but a localized skin reaction.

Incidence: Spider bites are common, but serious injury from them is not. Nearly 10,000 bites are reported to poison control centers, and many bites are not reported. Black widow bites cause about three deaths a year in the United States. Brown recluse and tarantula bites are rarely fatal.

Noticeable symptoms: You may not even feel the actual bite of a black widow spider, but soon after severe pain begins. You will have flulike symptoms as your immune system reacts to the poison. As the toxin attacks your nerves, your chest or abdominal muscles will become rigid, and muscles in your arms and legs will begin to spasm. You may also have difficulty in breathing and swallowing.

The bite of a brown recluse or a hobo spider causes a large spreading sore. This may be accompanied by fever, chills, a rash or red spots, nausea, vomiting, weakness, and painful joints.

Tarantula bites usually produce only localized pain, swelling, redness, and itching. Sometimes they may also cause a fever.

Any spider bite can easily become infected with bacteria. Get treatment for persistent or spreading infection even if the spider is not of a type known to be poisonous.

Treatment options: For all spider bites the wound should be cleaned; a tetanus shot may be advisable since it is a puncture wound. Antivenin for black widow bites may be administered to children or elderly patients. For most others doctors may treat the symptoms instead, using muscle relaxants, morphine for pain, and other medications. Unless a patient is highly allergic to tarantula venom, no treatment is necessary beyond cleaning the wound and possibly administering a tetanus shot.

Prevention: Keeping in mind where spiders are likely to live can help prevent your being bitten. When moving things around in sheds, garages, and basements, wear a pair of heavy gloves. Do not reach into places that you cannot see.

Spina bifida

(SPIY-nuh BIHF-ih-duh)

DISEASE

TYPE: DEVELOPMENTAL

enlarged view of embryo approximately 3 weeks: neural folds fail to meet

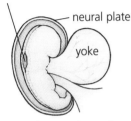

— neural plate

yoke

approximately 4 weeks: embryo continues to develop, but bone and muscle cannot protect nerves

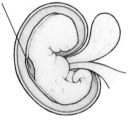

at birth: spinal cord may protude through malformed vertebrae

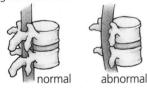

normal   abnormal

In the early embryo the neural tube, made up of the cells from which the brain and spinal cord develop, is formed from the neural plate. Sometimes the sides fail to join properly at some point. Bone and muscle tissue cannot grow across such a gap. If the gap occurs in the part that will become the spinal cord, the likely result will be spina bifida.

Spina bifida ("split spine") is also known as *open spine*. Normally, the vertebras form a column of complete, protective rings—the spinal column—around the spinal cord. In spina bifida one or more vertebras do not form completely, leaving an unprotected opening at the back of the spinal column.

Spina bifida is the most common of a group of disorders called neural tube defects. They originate within the first month of pregnancy. In the early embryo the neural tube is made up of the cells from which the brain and spinal cord will develop. It is formed in turn from a flat layer of cells called the neural plate; the sides of the plate curl up and fuse together. Sometimes the sides fail to join properly at some point along their length. Bone and muscle tissue, which would normally develop to protect the nerve tissue, cannot grow across such a gap. If the gap occurs in the part of the tube that will become the spinal cord, the likely result will be spina bifida.

Types: Spina bifida has three forms, which simply represent degrees of severity in the same basic defect:

Spina bifida occulta (uh-KULT-uh): This is the least serious form. The opening in the spinal column is so slight that it may not be outwardly noticeable (*occulta* means "hidden"). A birthmark or a patch of hair may appear directly over the opening, or fatty tissue may cause a small bulge or a dimple.

Spina bifida occulta usually causes no immediate health problems. But the lower end of the spinal cord may be attached, or "tethered," to the bones of the spinal column. As the afflicted child grows, the tethered cord may become stretched, causing some numbness in the legs or occasional loss of bladder control.

Meningocele: The term means "bulging of the meninges." Meninges are three-layered membranes that surround the brain and spinal cord. A meningocele occurs when the opening in one or more vertebras is extensive enough to allow the meninges to balloon through it.

The bulge produces a noticeable lump under the skin—it may be as small as a grape or as large as a grapefruit. If it contains only cerebrospinal fluid, it will not cause immediate harm. But if any of the nerves directly communicating with the spinal cord protrude into the sac, muscle weakness and some loss of bladder control may result.

Myelomeningocele: This word means "bulging of the meninges *and* the spinal cord." Myelomeningocele is the most common as well as the most severe form of the defect. It is also the one to which the general term spina bifida is often applied.

The sac protruding through the vertebral gap contains nerves as well as fluid. In the most serious cases the spinal cord comes to an end at this point. There is little or no skin over the sac; fluid may leak out of it; and inflamed sores may cover the area. As soon as the baby leaves the protective environment of the womb, infection becomes an immediate danger.

The higher in the spine a myelomeningocele occurs, and the more nerve tissue involved, the more body functions are affected. Below the swelling, sensation and motor control are limited and may virtually cease. Lack of sensation may cause imbalances in muscle groups, leading to deformations of the feet or spine or dislocation of the hips.

Most babies who have myelomeningocele also have hydrocephalus ("water on the brain"), which requires prompt treatment. Most children with this form of spina bifida also have some form of learning difficulty and about one in four have some degree of developmental disability (mental retardation).

Cause: The causes of all neural tube defects are unknown. They are probably at least partly genetic. They tend to be concentrated in certain ethnic groups and run in families.

Neural tube defects also occur more often than usual in children of mothers who have diabetes, who have had a high fever during early pregnancy, or who take the antiseizure drugs valproic acid or carbamazepine. Since the B vitamin folate seems to help prevent neural defects, it is presumed that a deficiency of this vitamin is among the causes.

Incidence: Spina bifida affects about 1 in 1,000 babies. About 90% are born with the most serious form, myelomeningocele. In addition, many affected fetuses are miscarried or stillborn.

Noticeable symptoms: The more serious forms, meningocele and myelomeningocele, are evident at birth. Spina bifida occulta may not be noticeable at all.

Diagnosis: A test of the mother's blood during pregnancy may reveal a chemical produced by the nervous system of the fetus. The presence of this chemical indicates almost surely that the fetus has some open neural tube defect (most likely myelomeningocele) from which the chemical has leaked. Spina bifida and the hydrocephalus that often accompanies it may also be visible by ultrasound examination during pregnancy. After birth diagnosis of all forms of the defect, including spina bifida occulta, can be confirmed by x-ray.

Treatment options: Spina bifida occulta may not need any immediate treatment at all. Surgery to close the gap in the spinal column or to release a "tethered" spinal cord may be advisable in childhood. Meningocele is more likely to justify surgery during infancy so as to improve the chances for healthy growth and reduce the risk of infection.

Myelomeningocele is almost always a medical emergency that requires surgery right after birth, if only to prevent infection. Any nerve tissue is put back in the spinal canal and covered with muscle and skin. Hydrocephalus usually requires the prompt insertion of a shunt (a valve to drain off fluid) as soon as the condition becomes apparent. Later, surgery or orthopedic treatment may be helpful in preventing or repairing deformations such as scoliosis or dislocated hips.

Outlook: Some children are only mildly affected. Others are seriously impaired and need mechanical aids and special training to move their legs and manage elimination.

Prevention: The vitamin folate appears to reduce by 50 to 70% the risk of all neural tube defects. Since half of all pregnancies are unexpected, a minimum dose of 400 micrograms (0.4 milligrams) a day is recommended for all women of childbearing age, and 800 micrograms a day for those who are either pregnant or intending to become so. Women who are considered at high risk, such as mothers of affected children, are urged to take 4,000 micrograms, or 4 milligrams, daily

To aid in the prevention of neural tube defects, a synthetic form of folate, folic acid, is now added to processed grain products in the United States. Some fortified breakfast cereals contain a full 400 micrograms per serving. For higher doses, folic acid tablets are readily available.

Spinal cord

BODY SYSTEM

The spinal cord is a vital part of the nervous system. It is connected to the base of the brain and transmits nerve impulses between the brain and all parts of the body. It is encased in the *spinal column,* the part of the skeleton running up the center of the back.

The spinal cord is surrounded by three protective membranes, called *meninges,* which extend around the brain as well. In appearance the spinal cord resembles a hollow tube within a tube. The outer tube is made up of nerve fibers with white sheaths called *myelin;* the inner tube is gray matter consisting mainly of nerve cell bodies. A central canal containing a lubricating liquid called *spinal fluid* runs up the center of the spinal cord and into the brain.

Size and location: Just under a half inch in diameter the

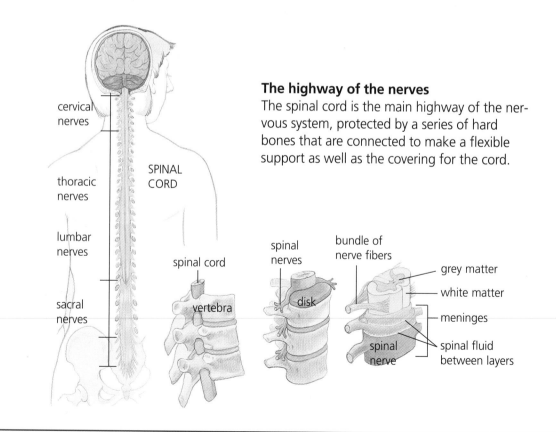

cervical nerves

thoracic nerves

lumbar nerves

sacral nerves

SPINAL CORD

spinal cord

vertebra

spinal nerves

disk

bundle of nerve fibers

grey matter

white matter

meninges

spinal nerve

spinal fluid between layers

The highway of the nerves
The spinal cord is the main highway of the nervous system, protected by a series of hard bones that are connected to make a flexible support as well as the covering for the cord.

spinal cord of an adult is some 16 to 18 inches long. It extends from the brain to approximately two-thirds of the way down the spinal column (to the first or second lumbar vertebra).

Function: The spinal cord is the brain's main communications link with the rest of the body. Nerve endings in various parts of the body feed sensations to the peripheral nerves, which in turn pass them on to the spinal cord and the brain. In turn, the brain sends commands (motor impulses) back down the spinal column and out the appropriate peripheral nerves, telling muscles to act or glands to secrete. Certain reflex actions, such as the sudden leg jerk produced by a tap just below the kneecap, are handled by the spinal cord without involving the brain.

Major malfunctions: Nearly 8,000 Americans injure their spinal cords each year. Any injury that breaks the spinal cord causes paralysis of all parts of the body controlled by that portion of the cord beyond the break. Such paralysis is usually permanent. Nerves in the spinal cord do not grow back together, although research is underway on repairing severed nerves using nerve growth factors and stem cells. Various back and spine problems, as well as malignant or benign tumors or malformations of vertebras, can interfere with normal functioning of the spinal cord by pressing on some portion of it. In rare cases babies are born with spina bifida, a condition in which the spinal cord is partly exposed, or other neural tube defects that occur during fetal development.

Spinal stenosis
(SPIY-nuhl steh-NOH-sihs)

DISORDER

TYPE: MECHANICAL

Spinal stenosis is a narrowing or constriction of the lower part of the spinal canal (the tunnel-like passage through the vertebras that contains the spinal cord and nerve roots). Narrowing of the canal can compress and injure the nervous tissue.

Cause: Spinal stenosis can be congenital or acquired. *Congenital stenosis* results from malformations that occur during development of a fetus and typically causes symptoms early in life. *Acquired stenosis* most often is caused by osteoarthritis and thus is a result of the aging process. Injuries, tumors, and infections such as *Paget's disease* also may cause spinal stenosis.

See also
Bone diseases
Osteoarthritis
Spinal cord

Phone doctor

Incidence: Congenital stenosis is relatively uncommon. Acquired stenosis is most common in middle-aged and elderly people. It occurs in about 5 out of 1,000 Americans over age 50.

Noticeable symptoms: As the nervous tissue is squeezed, the patient may feel numbness, pain, or a tickling sensation in the lower back, buttocks, thighs, or calves. The symptoms may occur on one or both sides of the body. They typically are strongest when the person is walking or exercising, often disappearing during periods of rest. The symptoms tend to become more severe over time. A person who experiences such symptoms should see a doctor. Early treatment improves the chances of a successful outcome.

Diagnosis: A diagnosis of spinal stenosis is based on physical and neurological examinations. An x-ray of the spine can reveal narrowing of the spinal canal, formation of bony spurs, and other degenerative changes. A CT scan or an MRI may be performed to confirm the diagnosis, particularly if surgery is being considered.

Treatment options: If symptoms are mild, therapy consists of an exercise program, including aerobic activities, and anti-inflammatory drugs. Overweight patients are urged to lose weight. If these steps are ineffective or if symptoms worsen, steroid injections into the affected area of the spine or surgery to reduce pressure on the nervous system may be recommended. Physical therapy may be needed following surgery.

Spleen

BODY SYSTEM

Although a person can live without a spleen—it is not a *vital organ*—the spleen has important functions in maintaining blood volume, cleaning blood, and providing immune protection.

Size and location: Although the spleen is like the heart in size and in its location on the left side of the body (but lower down, just behind the stomach), it weighs only about five or six ounces by itself. But in a living person it is nearly always filled with blood, perhaps as much as a quart, which brings its weight to over a pound. When there is a need, however, it can

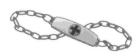

Medic alert

pump out almost all of that blood to improve blood pressure and general circulation.

Role: The spleen act as a cleaner and storehouse for blood. Especially, it removes damaged red blood cells and platelets along with bacteria, funguses, and viruses found in the blood. It also stores excess blood and red blood cells until they are needed.

The spleen also has an important role in the immune system, being the largest mass of lymphoid tissue in the body. It is sometimes thought of as the largest lymph node. Some lymphocytes, white blood cells such as B cells, are produced in the spleen. It can produce all types of blood cells in an emergency.

Conditions that affect the spleen: The various forms of polycythemia are disorders in which there are too many red blood cells. Since the spleen must deal with this overproduction, it may become enlarged. Other conditions that cause enlarged lymph nodes also may result in an enlarged spleen; these include leukemia, lymphomas, and Hodgkin's disease among the cancers.

Infections, such as mononucleosis, that enlarge lymph nodes also affect the spleen. In some instances mononucleosis has caused the spleen to enlarge so much that it bursts (*ruptures*).

Because it is well supplied with blood, a ruptured spleen can produce anemia if it loses blood slowly or shock if it loses blood rapidly. A ruptured spleen from an accident, such as an automobile accident, can result in death, sometimes when it seems that one has recovered from the effects of the accident. Emergency surgery is needed to correct the problems caused by a ruptured spleen.

Other diseases that result in enlargement of the spleen include brucellosis, cirrhosis of the liver, rheumatoid arthritis, typhoid fever, malaria, syphilis, and some types of anemia. For the most part, an enlarged spleen in these diseases is more important as a diagnostic tool than it is a danger to the patient.

The spleen sometimes shrinks in response to diseases, including autoimmune diseases, sprue, and sickle cell anemia. Persons whose spleen has atrophied or who have had their spleen removed are more susceptible to meningitis and pneumonia. They should be vaccinated against these diseases and wear a medic-alert bracelet to ensure proper treatment in case of fevers.

Spondylosis

See **Back and spine problems**

Spots before eyes

See also
Detached retina
Diabetes mellitus, type I ("juvenile")
Diabetes mellitus, type II ("adult-onset")
Eyes and vision
Head injuries

Phone doctor

Spots before the eyes (or stars or flashes of light before the eyes) may be due to a sharp rap on the head. They may also be due to harmless internal specks that float across your field of vision. These are also called *floaters.*

Parts affected: The kinds of spots caused by a blow last for only a few seconds and then disappear. Electrical nerve impulses in nature, these flashes are of no lasting significance so long as the blow to the head is not serious in itself.

Floaters are also trivial in most cases. These seem to move through the field of vision rapidly when the eye is moving but slow down when the eye is at rest. Floaters are produced by microscopic structures in the eye's inner fluid, termed the vitreous humor. They float in this jellylike substance that fills the central cavity of the eyeball, casting shadows on the retina at the back of the eye.

Almost everyone experiences floaters at one time or another, and almost always the specks disappear in time. They tend to increase in number and frequency among the elderly.

Associations: The sudden appearance of a cluster of dark floaters or showers of dark spots, however, can indicate a more serious problem. Such a cluster, especially if accompanied by bright flashes of light, is a possible sign of detached retina. *If you suddenly see a large number of black spots at once, get in touch immediately with an ophthalmologist.*

A single red floater of a size large enough to obscure vision is also a cause for concern. This indicates bleeding within the eye, which can result from diabetes mellitus.

Prevention and possible actions: Floaters that persist, that obscure vision, or that change in their behavior, as well as the showers of dark spots referred to above, are cause for immediate referral to an ophthalmologist.

Sprains

See **Fractures, dislocations, sprains, and strains**

Sprue

Sprue, or *celiac* (SEE-lee-AAK) *disease,* is a partly genetic, partly autoimmune disease of the digestive organs that varies widely in its severity and timing. A tropical infection that produces similar symptoms is also known as sprue, or *tropical sprue.* Some prefer to label the genetic, autoimmune disease as *celiac sprue.*

Cause: The immediate cause is an abnormal sensitivity to the proteins, together known as *gluten* (GLOOT-n), contained in wheat, rye, and barley (and probably oats, but *not* rice).

Sprue seems to be at least partly genetic—the disease is strongly familial. But more than one gene may be involved, and environmental factors as well. The symptoms of sprue stem from the immune system attacking part of the nutrient-absorbing apparatus of the small intestine, so it is classed as an autoimmune disease.

The lining of the small intestine becomes damaged, hindering at least somewhat its normal ability to absorb fats and other nutrients from food.

Incidence: Sprue is quite common in Italy (1 in 250) and in Ireland (1 in 300), which has led researchers to question the number of reported cases in the United States, which is about 1 in 4,700. Random studies of Americans, in fact, find many previously undiagnosed cases.

Noticeable symptoms: Symptoms may occur when a baby first starts eating solid food, but they may be delayed for years. The most evident symptom is persistent diarrhea. It may be accompanied or followed by signs of malnutrition or anemia. In adults one indication is unexplained weight loss. Infants may show failure to thrive and children may develop with short stature.

Since nutrients pass unabsorbed into the large intestine, they may provoke gas, cramps, and fatty diarrhea. Another consequence may be malnutrition, leading to retarded growth and vitamin and mineral deficiency disorders such as iron-deficiency anemia.

Diagnosis: A series of blood tests, x-rays, and a biopsy of the intestinal lining may be required. A blood test for antibodies to gluten is helpful, but a biopsy showing characteristic damage to the small intestine is most definitive.

Treatment options: All grain products except rice must be removed from the diet indefinitely. This may require special effort, since the offending proteins are used in many processed foods, from ice cream to salad dressing.

Outlook: If identified and treated promptly, sprue need not have any lasting negative effects. However, untreated sprue can lead to some forms of cancer, osteoporosis, miscarriage, congenital malformations, and seizures.

"Staph"
(STAAF)

DISEASE

TYPE: INFECTIOUS
(BACTERIAL)

See also
Bacteria and disease
Blister
Blood poisoning
Boils
Bone diseases
Diarrhea
Endocarditis
Eyes and vision
Food poisoning
Kawasaki disease
Nail infections and injuries
Nosocomial infections
Osteomyelitis
Pink eye
Pneumonia
Rashes
Skin diseases
Styes and chalazions
Toxic shock syndrome

Bacteria of the *Staphylococcus* group, commonly known as "staph," cause a wide range of serious, life-threatening diseases: toxic shock syndrome, abscesses, blood poisoning, a form of pneumonia, and most cases of infectious arthritis. Staph also causes many less serious conditions, including styes and pink eye, bloody diarrhea, and some food poisoning. Skin infections caused by staph bacteria range from boils and impetigo to *scalded skin syndrome*, a skin infection in babies and young children that causes extensive blisters.

Staph bacteria of the species *Staphylococcus aureus* are a very common cause of pus-filled boils, of infections of cuts and wounds in the skin, and of internal infections after surgery. They are also the source of most blood poisoning, of about 60% of all cases of osteomyelitis, and of toxic shock syndrome.

Cause: Staph bacteria attack parts of the body in a variety of ways. For example, once inside a cut they secrete toxic substances that dissolve tissue and enable the bacteria to penetrate further into the skin or other tissue. They may travel by the bloodstream from a simple cut or boil to cause devastating endocarditis or osteomyelitis.

Incidence: Almost every person at some time has had a minor staph infection of a cut. People with low resistance are at relatively high risk of developing a severe staph infection.

A number of surgical patients develop postoperative bacterial infections. Most of the nearly million American patients who did so in a recent year suffered from staph infection.

Treatment options: Treatment for different types of staph infection varies to a substantial extent according to the type of infection. In general, antibiotics prove effective for many types of the more severe staph infections. However, new strains of staph bacteria resistant to earlier antibiotics have evolved in recent years. In consequence physicians try to select newer antibiotics that are effective against the resistant strains.

Prevention: Use of antiseptic lotions or sprays on small cuts or abrasions can help keep staph from getting a foothold. Do not use antiseptics on deep cuts, however. They will not do much good and may give a false sense of security.

STD (sexually transmitted diseases)

REFERENCE

Sexually transmitted diseases (STDs), sometimes called *venereal diseases,* are usually passed through sexual activity. The most well known STDs—syphilis, gonorrhea, herpes, chlamydia—affect the genitals and reproductive system, but they can also harm other parts of the body, especially if they are untreated or improperly treated. Other diseases, including hepatitis B and hepatitis C, can be transmitted sexually, but often are transmitted in other ways. More than 20 diseases are known to be sexually transmitted. These include diseases caused by bacteria, protozoans, viruses, and funguses. Infestations of *crab lice,* small arthropods, can also be passed from person to person during sex.

In the 1980s people learned of a new and devastating STD, acquired immunodeficiency syndrome, or AIDS. This fatal disorder is caused by a virus known as the human immunodeficiency virus, or HIV. AIDS has been epidemic throughout the world since its discovery in the early 1980s.

Incidence: In the early 1990s more than 13 million Americans a year were affected by STDs. By the mid-1990s there was a decrease in cases of most STDs. This may be related to safe-sex messages and behavioral changes driven by the AIDS epidemic. In spite of this good news, the incidence of STDs remains high among adolescents and young adults. Two-thirds of the people affected by STDs are younger than 25, and many have had more than one STD. An estimated 25% of all sexually active 15-to-24-years-olds get an STD each year.

New STDs in the United States: Some STDs have emerged as new health problems. *Genital warts* are caused by any of 50 different strains of human papilloma virus (HPV). Different strains produce different looking warts. Some are flat, some are rough and raised, some are almost invisible, and some are quite large. They occur on the genitals and around the anus. The warts may result in itching of the affected area and, in women, vaginal discharge. They are removed by special lotions or surgery.

Three STDs that are common in tropical countries are now being seen in the United States.

- *Chancroid* (SHAANG-kroid), or soft chancre, starts as red-rimmed bacteria-filled sores or bumps on the genitals. These burst, releasing bacteria that spread, causing other sores and swollen lymph nodes in the groin. Symptoms occur within a week of infection; the bacteria can be passed to sexual partners as long as there are open sores. Chancroid can be cured with antibiotics.

- *Granuloma inguinale* (graan-yuh-LOH-muh ihng-gwuh-NAA-lay) is caused by a bacterial infection. It begins as a small blister on the genitals or near the anus, then enlarges into a raised red bump that gradually grows, destroying the tissue in its path. Antibiotics are used to cure granuloma.

- *Lymphogranuloma venereum (LGV)* is caused by several types of *Chlamydia,* but not the same type that causes the STD called genital chlamydia. It seems to be associated with anal intercourse. The disease begins as a sore on the genitals or around the anus one to three weeks after infection. The sore is painless, but the bacteria spread to the lymph nodes in the groin. The lymph nodes become painful as they swell with infection, burst, and drain through the skin above them. Treatment with antibiotics cures LGV.

Complications: Many STDs have serious consequences beyond the initial infection. If untreated, syphilis can lead to heart and brain damage and, in some cases, serious mental illness. Genital warts are associated with cervical cancer. Chlamydia infection is the major cause of PID (pelvic inflammatory disease) and sterility in women; it can also cause sterility in men. Gonorrhea can cause PID and sterility.

Many STDs are transmitted from mother to child as well as sexually. If a pregnant woman has an STD she can transmit it to

Sexually transmitted diseases often cause widespread havoc with many parts of the body. AIDS and untreated syphilis can produce dementia as well as many other symptoms. Some STDs are thought to lead to cancer. Others initiate male or female sterility. The child of an infected woman can also be harmed by some STDs.

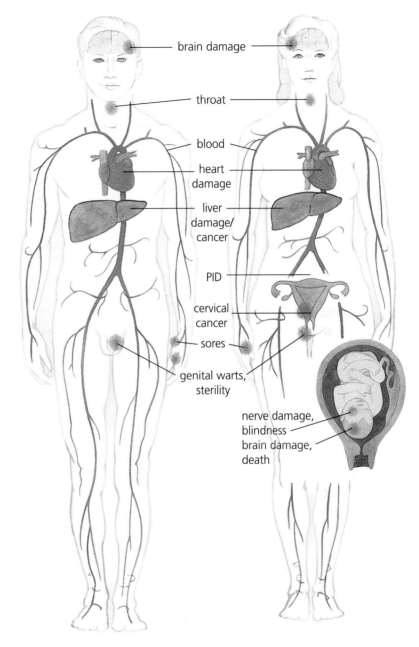

brain damage

throat

blood

heart damage

liver damage/ cancer

PID

cervical cancer

sores

genital warts, sterility

nerve damage, blindness brain damage, death

her baby either during pregnancy (syphilis and HIV, for example) or delivery (herpes and gonorrhea, for example). HIV can also be transmitted through breast-feeding. Untreated syphilis in babies can cause blindness and brain and nerve damage; HIV infection in babies leads to AIDS and, eventually, to death.

Prevention: There are no vaccinations to protect against most STDs, even though there has been considerable research aimed

Disease	Cause	Symptoms	Treatment
Chancroid	Bacterium	Red-rimmed sores; swollen lymph nodes	Antibiotics will cure; sores are drained surgically
Chlamydia	Bacterium	No symptoms at first; painful urination; discharge	Antibiotics will cure
Genital herpes	Virus	Bumps or sores on genitals or around anus	Antivirals will help keep in check; no cure
Genital warts	Virus	Painless dark bumps on genitals and around anus	Removal; no cure
Gonorrhea	Bacterium	Painful urination; discharge; abnormal menstruation	Antibiotics will cure
Granuloma inguinale	Bacterium	Raised red bumps that grow and spread, eating away at skin	Antibiotics will cure
HIV (AIDS)	Virus	No symptoms at first; early flulike symptoms; after 8–12 years compromised immune system	Antivirals; treatment of infections; no cure
Lymphogranuloma venereum	Bacterium	Painless sore; swollen glands that drain onto skin surface	Antibiotics will cure
Syphilis	Bacterium	Stage 1: Painless sore (chancre); stage 2: rash, swollen glands; stage 3: brain and heart damage	Antibiotics will cure
Trichomoniasis	Protozoan	No symptoms (men); vaginal discharge, painful urination (women)	Medications will cure
Vaginal yeast infection	Fungus	Vaginal discharge; itching	Medications will cure
Vaginitis	Bacterium; protozoan	Vaginal discharge; itching	Medications will cure

at developing such protection. The only STD for which there is an effective vaccination is hepatitis B. Since the mid-1990s babies have received hepatitis B vaccination as part of their routine immunization. It is recommended that everyone over 11 or 12 get the hepatitis B vaccination.

The only sure way to avoid STDs, other than hepatitis B, is to abstain from vaginal, anal, and oral sex. For most people abstinence is not a lifelong option, but individuals can delay the start of sexual relations until some measure of maturity is achieved.

After abstinence the best safe-sex practice is using a condom correctly every time with every partner. A male condom is

Get vaccinated

a latex sheath used to cover a man's penis during the sex act, including anal and oral sex. The newer female condom fits inside the vagina. Condom use is not foolproof, but it can decrease the transmission of STDs dramatically.

Reduce the number of sex partners. The more partners a person has, the greater the likelihood of having sex with someone with an STD and of becoming infected.

Stem cells

Imagine a time when illnesses such as diabetes and Parkinson's disease can be cured by replacing defective cells with healthy ones, when damaged heart muscle can be replaced by healthy tissue, and replacement organs are readily available for transplant. Scientists around the world are studying and doing research with special human cells that may make all of these examples realities. These special cells are called stem cells. Unlike most body cells, which are very specialized, stem cells have the ability to grow into many different types of cells and tissues.

Sources of stem cells: The term "stem cells" was originally applied to cells in bone marrow that produce blood cells. A group of cells produced by a particular stem cell is called a line. This is still one meaning of the term "stem cell," but more recently it has also come to mean any cells that can reproduce a line of cells of a particular type, and especially generalized cells that can be encouraged to develop into different lines by different treatments. These generalized stem cells come from three sources: embryos, blood from the umbilical cord when a baby is born, and adults.

Embryonic stem cells are the first cells that are formed when a sperm fertilizes an egg and cell division begins. If the earliest cells are separated, they have the ability to form all of the different types of cells in a human and even grow into a whole person. As the cells continue to divide, they begin to lose some of their ability to form all possible types of cells, but they can still form a large number of cell types.

Stem cells from blood from the umbilical cord that have not taken up a final specialty can grow into a smaller number of types of cell lines. Adult stem cells are cells from adults that, like the bone-marrow stem cells that produce blood cells, are the basis of cell lines of various types.

Researchers value embryonic stem cells the most since they have the ability to form any kind of cell in the body. Although a fertilized egg after the first few cell divisions is only the size of the period at the end of this sentence, growing the fertilized egg in a ball of cells is done in a petri dish, and all the cells can be used. Ethicists have questioned using such techniques to create stem cells, however, since a fertilized egg, if successfully implanted in a human uterus, can develop into a complete human.

Adult stem cells are harder to find in the body, so thousands or even millions of cells may have to be screened before the stem cells can be found. An additional challenge with adult stem cells is finding the stem cells that will grow into the type of cells that are needed: Different adult stem cells only grow into a small number of types of cells.

Stem cell research: Some think that the treatment of almost every human disease might be improved if stem cell research is successful. Most stem cell research is being done on diseases affecting only a single type of cell. Diabetes and Parkinson's disease are two current research targets. In diabetes insulin-producing cells no longer function properly. Stem cell research is attempting to create these cells so that healthy cells can be put in the body and produce insulin. For Parkinson's disease stem cell research would create new brain cells and replace the cells that result in the disease.

Scientists are also looking at ways to use stem cells to treat other disease conditions, including replacing heart tissue damaged during a heart attack and replacing bone marrow cells destroyed during chemotherapy for cancer. Stem cell research has generated interest and hope among people paralyzed by spinal cord injuries. Stem cells have been coaxed into growing into the type of nerve cells found in the spinal cord and may someday be used to treat or even cure spinal cord injuries.

One of the greatest hopes of stem cell research is that someday scientists will be able to create entire organs. Today there are long lists of people waiting for donated organs; many die before a suitable organ becomes available. If new organs could be produced using stem cells, replacement organs would be more available for people who need them.

Stem cell treatment in humans: New cells are placed in the body by injection or surgery, depending on the type of cell being replaced. Rejection of the new cells has to be prevented just as in an organ transplant. Finally, the new cells must function properly to correct the defect.

Although all stem cell treatment is experimental at this time, there has been some success. Researchers in Chicago are treating severe cases of Crohn's disease using stem cell technology. Crohn's disease is an inflammation of the digestive system caused when the body's immune system attacks the digestive system. Stem cells are collected from the patient's bone marrow and the immune system is destroyed. Then the patient's stem cells are put back into the body to create a new immune system. The desired outcome is that the new immune system will form properly and will not attack the digestive system.

This treatment is risky. During the few weeks the new immune system is developing, the patient must be kept in a sterile environment to prevent infection because any infection could be fatal. Regular medical follow-up visits are essential and may be necessary for life.

Similar techniques are being used successfully with certain cancers.

Stings

INJURY

A sting is a wound made by certain animals when a sharp body part called a *stinger* enters the body and injects a poison called *venom*. Most stings are minor annoyances—painful for a few moments but soon forgotten. However, people with known allergies to stings must be treated immediately to prevent shock.

Stings vary greatly in their poisonous effects. The sting of a domestic *honeybee* is not usually as unpleasant as that of a *hornet*. In some parts of the world the sting of a *scorpion* can be fatal, but scorpions in the western United States are not so toxic.

Cause: When certain insects or scorpions are disturbed or are looking for food, they may sting with a pointed stinger attached to their posterior end. The stinger injects venom. As the venom gets into the body, it causes a response by the immune system. Usually, the immediate area gets swollen as blood carrying immune cells come to the area to fight the irritating chemicals in the venom.

Emergency Room

Some *rays,* which are related to sharks and skates, have venomous barbs that can inflict wounds; these animals are called *stingrays.* Some marine invertebrates such as *jellyfish* and *sea urchins* have stinging tentacles or spines. Even some plants are equipped with stinging cells that cause injury when touched.

Incidence: Most insect stings occur outdoors in warm weather when insects are more likely to be numerous. Stings from marine animals such as rays, jellyfish, and sea urchins are likely to occur where people are swimming in warm water.

Noticeable symptoms: The usual reaction to a sting is sharp pain, then redness, itching, swelling, and a feeling of warmth around the sting for the first few hours. *However, if a person has a known severe reaction to a previous sting or begins to show signs of having difficulty breathing, medical help must be sought immediately.* Bee stings can cause a person with allergies to go into shock in as little as ten minutes. Also, if a person is stung in the mouth or throat area, the swelling may impair breathing, and medical attention may be required.

Treatment options: Most stings can be treated without medical evaluation, but treatment should begin immediately. The stinger and venom sac of a bee or *wasp* should be removed by scraping it out rather than pulling on it. If you have an *ant* sting, rinse it out with ammonia. Household ammonia is strongly alkaline and helps to neutralize the formic acid produced by ants. Wasps and hornets have an alkaline poison, so household acids such as vinegar or lemon juice help to remove their toxins and reduce pain.

Wash the sting area with soap and water and apply an antiseptic to kill germs. To reduce pain and swelling, use an ice pack, a cortisone cream, or a paste of sodium bicarbonate, for bee stings especially. Meat tenderizer can also be useful since it breaks down the proteins in the toxins. Taking antihistamines also reduces swelling. For stings on the hands be sure to remove rings immediately in case the fingers become very swollen.

Stings by marine animals are treated differently. If you are stung by jellyfish or sea urchins in the ocean, wash the sting area with alcohol with vinegar added to it rather than water. (If alcohol is not immediately available, rubbing sand against the skin

Emergency Room

Medic alert

in the sting area can remove toxins and prevent painful swelling, but may cause skin abrasion.) ***Anyone with a Portuguese-man-of-war sting or that of a stingray should get medical attention as these can be serious and require medication.***

Prevention: When spending time outdoors, especially in wooded environments where there are stinging insects, wear shoes and socks, long pants, and long sleeves. Apply a safe insect repellent in exposed areas. Avoid perfume that may attract stinging insects. If you are at a beach, be sure to heed warnings of jellyfish in the area, and stay out of the water when so advised.

If you have an allergy to stings, do not hike or swim alone. Wear a medic-alert bracelet describing your condition, and keep a self-care kit containing antihistamines and epinephrine. Such kits can be prescribed by your physician.

Stomach

BODY SYSTEM

See also
Adrenal glands
Anemias
Cancers
Diaphragm
Digestive system
Esophagus
Gastritis
Gastroenteritis
Stomachache
Ulcers
"Virus" infection

The stomach is sometimes called the belly, but this is inaccurate. *Belly* really refers to the region in the body between the ribs and pelvis that is more formally called the abdomen. The stomach is an important wide place in the digestive tract where food is held for a time before continuing with digestion. With valves at each end to keep food in place for three to five hours, the stomach churns like a washing machine, bathing food in acids and powerful enzymes that kill traveling bacteria and parasites as they break the food into a nearly featureless mush. Digestion proceeds when this material is released to the upper part of the small intestine, where additional enzymes attack it.

Size and location: The stomach is located in the upper part of the abdomen, below the diaphragm. The esophagus passes through the diaphragm, bringing chopped food from the mouth to the stomach.

The stomach is a pouch that can hold about a quart and a half of food at a time in an average adult.

Role: This organ produces enzymes (and therefore acts as a gland) and hydrochloric acid. These are mixed with food by the churning motion of the stomach, which tends to further break the food into smaller particles even as the stomach enzymes and acids are chemically changing the food. From this point forward this soup of nutrients is no longer referred to as food but as *chyme* (KIYM) as it moves through the intestines.

Conditions that affect the stomach: A stomachache, most often caused by problems in digestion, is familiar to everyone, although children suffer from it most as a result of smaller stomachs and less well-developed systems. Stomachache includes *indigestion* that comes whenever the stomach is irritated, perhaps by too much food. More serious problems are called gastritis (the word *gastric* means "stomach"), or inflammation of the stomach lining. This may be so severe as to cause vomiting to rid the stomach of its contents. A virus may cause gastritis as part of the viral infection gastroenteritis.

Certain chemicals used as medicines are known to affect the lining of the stomach adversely, notably aspirin and steroids. The same kind of *gastric erosion* is among the symptoms of the disorder of the adrenal glands known as *Addison's disease.*

Persistent stomachache in an adult is likely caused by *gastric ulcers.* Although ulcers are painful because of reactions with strong stomach fluids on sores lining the stomach, scientists now know that the sores themselves are caused by bacteria. Stress can induce a painful ulcer attack because it releases stomach fluids when food is not necessarily present.

People with *pernicious anemia* and some genetic conditions have diminished hydrochloric acid in their stomachs. This *achlorhydria* (AY-klawr-HIY-dree-uh) is not serious since digestion can proceed, although less efficiently, without the acid; but anemia that may be the root cause needs treatment.

The stomach is subject to cancer, but this is not especially common in the United States. Stomach cancer is more common in Japan, where the cause is thought to be salted and pickled foods that are abundant in the traditional Japanese diet.

Stomachache

A stomachache is a common symptom. But, despite the name, the stomachache is often caused by distress somewhere other than the stomach.

Parts affected: A stomachache is a pain somewhere in the

Call ambulance

Drink water

Phone doctor

area of the abdomen. Exercise or strain can cause superficial muscular pain that generally goes away on its own. Deeper pain in the upper abdomen may indicate an ailment of the stomach or gallbladder (gallbladder pain is also felt in the back). A deep pain in the lower abdomen (below the navel) might indicate an infection in the intestines or appendix.

Related symptoms: Stomachache may be accompanied by indigestion, constipation, diarrhea, nausea, vomiting, or fever. Chronic stomachache may signal a serious disorder and should be checked by a physician.

Associations: It is helpful to identify the cause of a particular stomachache to determine if it can be properly treated at home or whether medical assistance is required. Often the best clue is the other symptoms that accompany the ache in the belly.

■ *Appendicitis* can be life-threatening. It is characterized by pain that seems to begin at the navel and move to the lower right. It is sometimes, but not always, accompanied by vomiting. If an infected appendix bursts, peritonitis may occur. This condition is characterized by extremely sharp pain and a hard abdomen, rapid breathing, and high fever. It can be fatal.

■ *Constipation* is characterized by hard stools or the inability to have a bowel movement, but it also can cause abdominal pain. Usually this common ailment is easily remedied by using a fiber laxative or a stool softener.

■ *Diarrhea* is the condition of having recurrent watery stools. This may be caused by stress or by a diet containing too much high-fiber food. However, if accompanied by stomach cramps and weakness, diarrhea can indicate a viral or bacterial infection such as a stomach "flu" (viral gastroenteritis). It is important to prevent dehydration when this condition occurs, especially in the young. Replenish fluids and eat a bland diet, including binding foods such as bananas, rice, applesauce, and toast.

■ *Diverticulitis* is an inflammation of the small cavities within the intestines. This disease may cause muscle spasms and pain in the lower left abdomen. Antibiotics and pain relievers may be needed to get rid of infection and relieve discomfort.

■ *Food poisoning* is most common as a result of eating under-

Phone doctor

Irritable bowel syndrome
Lactose intolerance
Migraine
Peritonitis
Stomach
Ulcers

Phone doctor

cooked meat, poultry, or eggs. Usually, the other symptoms are nausea, vomiting, and diarrhea. In most cases home care is sufficient.

■ *Gallstones* are hard pellets usually made of cholesterol that clog the gallbladder or the ducts that connect it with the liver. More women than men, especially older women, experience characteristic sharp pains in the upper right abdomen and in the back. Surgery is recommended to relieve the symptoms.

■ *Indigestion* associated with pain in the upper abdomen may be a case of heartburn, a reaction to a specific food such as coffee, beans, citrus, or spices. Indigestion can also be a reaction to eating too much or too quickly or to taking in too much air when swallowing; antacid remedies can overcome this pain. Indigestion may also indicate a reaction to medication, traveler's diarrhea, diabetes mellitus, or lactose intolerance.

■ *Irritable bowel syndrome* causes pain in the mid to lower abdominal area and is accompanied by bloating, gas, headache, and fatigue.

■ *Migraine* is usually thought of as a headache, but in many cases it is accompanied by stomachache as well.

■ *Peptic ulcer* is injury to the stomach or upper small intestine caused by the erosive action of digestive enzymes and acids on sores in the lining. Its symptoms include burning, gnawing pain after eating, and black stool, which indicates that the ulcer is bleeding and needs medical attention.

"Strep"

DISEASE

TYPE: INFECTIOUS (BACTERIAL)

The bacteria of the family known formally as *Streptococcus* and more commonly as "strep" are, along with *Staphylococcus,* or "staph," one of the main causes of human disease. Strep causes scarlet fever and rheumatic fever, many cases of blood poisoning, a form of heart disease, some cases of kidney disease, most tonsillitis, some cases of toxic shock syndrome, and the skin disease *erysipelas.* A child home from school because of a fever and a painful red throat should be checked for *strep throat,* which is perhaps the most common symptom of a strep infection. All these diseases are caused by the bacteria called Group A *Streptococcus.* These are also the "flesh-eating bacteria" that cause *necrotizing fasciitis* (NEHK-ruh-tiyz-ing FAASH-ee-IY-tihs).

Cause: Streptococcus bacteria produce chemicals or toxins that irritate or even kill the cells that line the throat or other tissues. As the body's immune system attempts to force out these intruding bacteria, more and more blood goes to the irritated area, making it appear extremely red. If flesh has been killed, however, blood cannot reach the area.

Incidence: Nearly 10,000 cases of strep infection occur annually. Only a few hundred are either strep toxic shock syndrome or necrotizing fasciitis, the two most invasive strep diseases—half of the cases of strep toxic shock and 20% of necrotizing fasciitis become fatalities.

Noticeable symptoms: A sick feeling, a red throat, a fever of 101°F or higher, and painful swallowing are common symptoms of strep throat. Some children have convulsions or nausea. Some show no symptoms at all. If there is also a rash, the disease may be scarlet fever. Strep toxic shock begins with dizziness and confusion, fever, and a rash.

Phone doctor

Diagnosis: If a strep infection is suspected, it should be checked by a physician. Newer tests for detecting the bacteria make it possible for a physician to find out the result instantly instead of waiting for an overnight throat culture to develop.

Treatment options: To cure strep throat, antibiotics such as penicillin or its relatives are almost always prescribed to get rid of the bacteria completely. Although the course of antibiotics lasts for ten days, symptoms begin to disappear within 24 to 48 hours. However, anyone treated for the disease should always take the full prescription so that the bacteria do not return. To relieve symptoms, gargle with salt water and drink a mixture of tea, lemon, and honey. Drink cold liquids or suck on popsicles, but not in citrus flavors, which may make the throat feel worse. For pain, take aspirin substitute. ***Children and teenagers should not take aspirin because of the possibility of Reye's syndrome.*** Also, use lozenges that contain benzocaine to relieve throat pain.

Gargle saltwater

Avoid aspirin

Once the bacteria have infected the throat, the symptoms of a red and sore throat begin to appear. If untreated, the streptococcus infection can become scarlet fever, rheumatic fever, or glomerulonephritis, a severe kidney infection. These complications are discussed below:

- *Glomerulonephritis:* The actual damage is thought to be caused by antibodies directed against the bacteria, not by the bacteria themselves. With proper treatment most victims (usually children) recover completely, although permanent kidney damage can occur.
- *Rheumatic fever:* A strep infection that invades the joints and heart is called rheumatic fever. Although the disease has been reduced in incidence recently, probably because of antibiotics, children and young adults are still susceptible. The name stems from the pain and swelling in the joints, but the permanent damage comes from an infection of the valves of the heart, which occurs in about three infections out of five. Sometimes the brain is also affected by the bacterium, but the damage there is not permanent.
- *Scarlet fever:* This now rare strep-induced childhood disease is characterized by a high fever and distinctive rash.

Prevention: To prevent strep throat, wash your hands frequently and avoid close contact with people who have it.

Wash hands

Stroke

DISEASE

TYPE: MECHANICAL

When a person has a stroke, the supply of blood to the brain has been blocked, or blood has leaked into brain tissue. Brain cells in the affected area die, often resulting in serious permanent damage. Prompt medical attention can increase survival chances and can minimize the amount of disability.

Cause: There are three main causes of stroke.

About 75% of strokes are caused by blood clots. In *cerebral thrombosis* (SEHR-uh-bruhl throm-BOH-sihs) a clot forms in one of the arteries leading to the brain, often a carotid (kuh-ROT-ihd) artery. Cells in the affected part of the brain do not get an adequate supply of oxygen, sugar, and other blood nutrients. They quickly die. Cerebral thrombosis is most common in older people who have high blood pressure and clogged arteries.

In *cerebral embolism* the clot forms in some other part of the body, usually the heart. The clot or part of it breaks loose and travels through the bloodstream to the brain.

Most other strokes are caused by bleeding in the brain. This is known as *cerebral hemorrhage.* Blood may seep slowly into

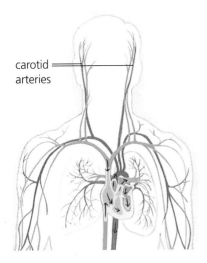

carotid
arteries

A stroke is damage to brain cells caused by blocked carotid arteries or by clogged or burst arteries in the brain.

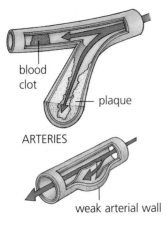

blood
clot

plaque

ARTERIES

weak arterial wall

Call ambulance

Phone doctor

brain tissue from a weakened artery. Or an artery may burst. A cerebral hemorrhage usually occurs in people with a long history of high blood pressure. It may also result from an aneurysm or an injury to the head. Although cerebral hemorrhage is less common than thrombosis or embolism, it is more likely to be fatal.

Incidence and risk factors: Every year about a half million Americans suffer a stroke. It is the third leading cause of death in the United States and the leading cause of serious disability. More than 70% of strokes occur in people over 65. Most victims have high blood pressure and atherosclerosis. Deadly strokes are more common in women than in men. They are three to four times more common in African Americans. People who have already had a stroke are more likely to have another. Cigarette smoking doubles the chances of having a stroke. Other risk factors include diabetes, family history, obesity, high cholesterol, and lack of exercise.

Noticeable symptoms: Often the victim experiences weakness, numbness, or paralysis of the face or an arm or leg, usually on one side of the body. There may also be difficulty in speaking or dimmed, blurred vision, usually in one eye, causing double vision. A sudden, very severe headache, discomfort with bright lights, dizziness, and loss of balance or loss of consciousness are other signs of stroke. *If you have any of these symptoms, summon an ambulance to take you to the hospital.*

Even if the symptoms last only a brief time and then disappear, you should see your physician. You may be having a TIA (transient ischemic attack), or ministroke. A TIA is a warning that you may have a stroke at any time in the future.

Diagnosis: A CT scan or an MRI of the brain can show whether the stroke was caused by a clot or a hemorrhage and where damage has occurred. There may be an ultrasound scan to locate blockages in the carotid arteries or problems originating in the heart. An arteriogram may be necessary. In this test a dye is inserted into the cerebral arteries, and a series of x-rays is taken.

Treatment options: Treatment will be directed at stopping the stroke's progress, limiting brain cell death, and preventing another stroke. For a stroke caused by an embolism, drugs will be used to help dissolve clots or prevent new clots. Surgery may be required to remove plaque from clogged carotid arteries or to remove a clot. For a cerebral hemorrhage treatment is entirely different; blood thinners or clot dissolvers may make the situation worse. Surgery is used to stop the bleeding.

Stages and progress: Stroke often worsens over a period of days. Brain cells continue to die, and physical and mental functions continue to decline. It is not unusual for a second stroke or a heart attack to occur during this period. It can be weeks before improvement begins. In about one-fourth of all strokes there is good recovery with no lasting damage. In half of all strokes there is permanent disability. Many strokes are fatal.

Prevention: You can best prevent a stroke by keeping risk factors under control. Have your blood pressure checked regularly, and treat it if it is high. Eat a low-fat diet, and follow an exercise program. If you are at high risk, your physician may have you take low-dose aspirin daily to prevent blood clots.

Cigarette smoking is another important factor that can lead to strokes. The nicotine in cigarettes causes blood platelets to get sticky and more likely to clot. It also contributes to high blood pressure. In addition, the amount of oxygen reaching the brain is reduced by the carbon monoxide in cigarette smoke.

Eat low-fat foods   Exercise

Don't smoke

Styes and chalazions

(kuh-LAY-zee-uhns)

DISEASE

TYPE: INFECTIOUS
(BACTERIAL);
MECHANICAL

A stye is a small abscess that forms on the leading edge of an eyelid. A chalazion is a round, painless swelling of the eyelid in which infection is not a factor. Both occur in children and teens more frequently than in adults.

Cause: A stye, also known as a *hordeolum* (hawr-DEE-uh-luhm), is a pimplelike infection often marked by a yellowish head. The infection, which is caused by bacteria, occurs in the glands that lie adjacent to the follicle, or root, of one of the eyelashes along the edges of the upper and lower eyelids. These glands secrete an oily substance that normally keeps the lashes soft, but they are vulnerable to the entry of infectious material, particularly if an individual is in the habit of rubbing his or her eyes with hands that have recently touched the nose or mouth.

Staphylococcus bacteria are among the more common triggers of styes, though other bacteria may have the same effect. Styes are found most often near the inside corners of the eyes, probably because this is the spot most often touched.

A chalazion, from the Greek word for "small hailstone," also involves an oil-producing gland, but in this instance the swelling arises as a result of internal blockage. Unable to exit the gland, the secretions build up within, gradually causing the gland and the covering eyelid to swell. If the swelling is allowed to grow to any size, it can exert pressure on the cornea at the front of the eye. Chalazions are particularly common in people who also experience such skin disorders as acne, rosacea, severe dandruff, and seborrheic dermatitis, all of which seem to involve blocked glands just below the skin's surface.

Noticeable symptoms: With a stye you will probably observe some localized swelling, a small pimple with perhaps a yellowish center, and in a matter of hours to days, a small discharge of pus. Pain and irritation are usual accompaniments of a developing stye, but these are likely to subside after the discharge.

In the instance of a chalazion the swelling may be somewhat larger and redder and show no evidence of a head. With sufficient pressure on the eye vision can become slightly blurred temporarily, and, for the same reason, a small amount of temporary astigmatism can result.

Treatment options: A stye usually does not need a physician's attention. Warm compresses may help the pus to discharge sooner, but the condition is likely to cure itself in a matter of days without any treatment. Care must be taken, however, not to transfer the infection from the stye to other sites on the same eye or on the other eye, so it is important to maintain especially clean hands and to avoid rubbing the eyes.

A stye that persists, or one that recurs often, indicates a visit to the doctor or ophthalmologist, who will probably prescribe antibiotic ointment and a change in personal habits. A biopsy may be taken to rule out cancer.

About one-third of chalazions disappear on their own. Another third can be cured with warm compresses for ten minutes four times a day. Large cysts may need to be opened and drained surgically under a local anesthetic.

Sunburn

INJURY

See also
Burns and scalds
Melanoma
Skin
Skin cancers

Whether on a beach or snow skiing on a sunny slope, even on an overcast day, fair-skinned people may experience sunburn. Applying a sunscreen to the skin can prevent sunburn and decrease the likelihood of getting skin cancer.

Cause: Sunburn occurs when the skin is overexposed to the ultraviolet (UV) rays of the sun.

Incidence: Infants and young fair-skinned children are at the greatest risk for getting sunburn because their skin is thinner and more sensitive to the sun.

Noticeable symptoms: Unfortunately, the symptoms of sunburn may not show up until several hours after being overexposed to the sun's rays. If the sunburn is minor, the skin turns pink or red. A more severe sunburn causes the skin to blister. There may be pain and a burning sensation in the affected areas. This may be followed by itching as the sunburned skin begins peeling off, usually in about a week. If a child seems overly sensitive to light, it may mean that he or she experienced sunburn on the cornea of the eye.

Treatment options: To reduce pain, ibuprofen or other analgesics are effective. A cool bath with a small amount of baking soda may also help with pain, as showers can cause a stinging sensation. Cortisone cream applied several times a day (especially on the first day) may reduce swelling.

Stages and progress: Every time a person gets a blistering sunburn, it doubles the risk of developing a serious type of skin cancer called malignant melanoma or a less serious form of skin cancer. Although skin cancer is more likely to occur in adults, it is caused by sunburns that occur during childhood. An intense sunburn must be treated as a second-degree burn.

Repeated exposure to the sun over time can cause the skin to wrinkle and sag prematurely.

Prevention: Until recently, physicians believed that sunscreens with a sun protection (SPF) of 15 or higher would prevent not only sunburn but also skin cancer. The evidence today suggests that while a sunscreen with a rating of at least SPF 15 will prevent sunburn, it may not prevent all the damage that can lead

Clothing screens out some of the sun, and, even better, a broad-brimmed hat helps protect facial skin from sunburn. Use of a sunscreen with an SPF greater than 15 and zinc oxide as an ingredient is also helpful.

to skin cancer. Sunscreens that contain zinc oxide, which blocks the sun's rays completely, provide the most protection from sunburn and also from cancer. When the sun is most intense, it is a good idea to stay in the shade.

Swellings

Swellings are enlargements of parts of the body that result from injury, disease, or other unusual change in bodily condition. They are most often temporary.

Parts affected: In most cases swellings appear on or just under the skin. They can develop in any of the soft tissues of the body, however, although swellings in the internal organs may be apparent only in the course of surgery.

Associations: In everyday experience swellings result most commonly from injuries, diseases, or allergies. Bruises caused by some object striking the skin are probably the most frequent form of swellings. Bleeding under the skin following the impact causes the typical features of a bruise—swelling and the blue-black and yellowish discoloration. Trauma to muscles, tendons, or ligaments often produces swelling whether there is bruising or not. But many other types of injuries also result in swellings. Among them are burns, frostbite, muscle cramps, radiation overexposures, and wounds. Stings, spider bites, and insect bites produce relatively small swellings, while poisonous snakebites or scorpion bites can produce large swellings quite rapidly. Allergies can produce hives but also the dangerous *anaphylactic shock*. One symptom of anaphylactic shock is sudden swelling of the tongue and face after exposure to insect venom or another allergen.

For some diseases swellings represent the most obvious symptom. Mumps, for instance, is almost always recognized by the prominent swellings of salivary glands on the sides of the neck. In tonsillitis badly swollen tonsils clearly appear. Cirrhosis of the liver (due almost always to alcoholism) eventually swells the liver to the point that its distension can very easily be detected by touch. Abscesses of the teeth sometimes grow so large that they appear as painful swellings of the jaw. Infections can produce unmistakably swollen boils on the skin. The rare disease *amyloidosis* (AAM-uh-loi-DOH-sihs), which produces amyloid protein deposits throughout the body, has swollen hands and feet as one symptom. The dramatic swelling of elephantiasis is caused by a parasitic worm.

Edema represents a special type of swelling. It results from an accumulation of fluid in the tissues where the swelling occurs, often in the legs or around the ankles. It has a variety of causes, including heart or kidney disease, the complication of pregnancy called preeclampsia, injury, or infection.

Relief of symptoms: Treatment appropriate to the underlying condition should be used to relieve whatever variety of swelling a person may have. Such treatment should be sought from a physician if the swelling persists for more than a few days, especially if it is accompanied by other symptoms such as pain or fever.

Swellings due to bruises, strains, or sprains may be relieved by applying an ice bag or a cloth soaked in cold water to the area for a few minutes at a time.

Mild cases of edema can be cleared up by physicians with the prescription of diuretic drugs.

Syphilis
(SIHF-uh-lihs)

DISEASE

TYPE: INFECTIOUS (BACTERIAL; SEXUALLY TRANSMITTED)

See also
**AIDS (acquired immunodeficiency
 syndrome)**
Bacteria and disease
Mental illnesses
Paralysis
Pregnancy and disease
Rashes
Reproductive system
STD (sexually transmitted diseases)
Yaws

The disease was spreading like wildfire, doctors could not cure it, and people shunned those who had it. AIDS? No, syphilis in sixteenth-century Europe. No one knows where or when syphilis began, but it has affected sexually active individuals in every part of the world for many centuries.

Cause: The bacterium *Treponema pallidum* causes syphilis when it enters the body during sexual contact. A pregnant woman infected with the bacterium can pass it to her developing fetus; the baby will be born with congenital syphilis.

Incidence: During the 1990s the rate of syphilis in the United States declined by 88%, with fewer than 6,000 cases in 2000. The national syphilis control program has been so effective that the Centers for Disease Control and Prevention is pursuing the goal of syphilis eradication in the United States by 2005. Achieving this goal would be an important health victory because of syphilis's fatal long-term effects and the harm it can cause to babies that are born with it.

Noticeable symptoms: The first symptom is a red, painless sore called a *chancre* (SHAANG-kuhr) that occurs where the bacteria entered the body. The sore can occur any place a person's body is touched during sex, but it is usually found on or in the genitals. Later symptoms include a rash on the palms of the hands, the soles of the feet, and all other parts of the body. The rash may be accompanied by fatigue, fever, swollen glands, and sore throat.

Diagnosis: A physician will perform an examination for sores and other signs of sexually transmitted disease. If syphilis is suspected, a blood test is used to confirm the diagnosis.

Treatment options: Antibiotics are effective in treating syphilis. It is important that all partners are tested and treated at the same time so the bacteria are not passed back and forth. Doing this avoids having a treated partner reinfected by an infected untreated partner. If the person is also HIV-infected, special treatment may be needed.

Stages and progress: Syphilis progresses in three stages. Stage one begins with the chancre, which usually appears three to four weeks after infection. The chancre will go away without treatment, but the bacteria are still in the body. Six weeks to six months after the chancre first appears, stage two begins with a rash (often on the palms and soles of the feet), hair loss, swollen glands, fever, and other flulike symptoms. The symptoms of this stage will go away in two to six weeks if untreated. The bacteria are not gone, however. Years later, in stage three, serious health problems occur. Late-stage syphilis can result in severe damage to the heart and blood vessels. It can infect the brain and cause paralysis, blindness, and dementia or insanity. It can even cause death.

Untreated syphilis during pregnancy can cause deformities in the baby or, in some cases, death. Widespread public health regulations require that all babies be tested for syphilis right after birth and that those who are infected be given treatment immediately.

Prevention: Syphilis is passed from an infected to an uninfected person during sex. Any person with a syphilitic sore can transmit the bacteria to a sexual partner. Transmission can occur many years after the person carrying syphilis first became infected. The sores can be inside the body, so it is often impossible to tell by looking.

The surest prevention is to abstain from sex. The next best

prevention is to use condoms during each and every sexual encounter. Limiting the number of sex partners reduces the chance of having sex with someone who is infected. However, even in a monogamous relationship, if one person has untreated syphilis, the other partner is likely to become infected.

Pregnant women should have a blood test for syphilis at least once during pregnancy. If they are infected it is important for them to be treated, then retested to be sure that the syphilis has been cured. This is necessary to prevent passing the bacteria to the developing fetus.

Tapeworm

DISEASE

TYPE: PARASITIC

See also
Anemias
Diarrhea
Digestive system
Parasites and disease

A tapeworm is a parasitic flatworm that lives in the intestines. Tapeworms are found in nature worldwide and can infest many different kinds of animals. Tapeworms are passed on to humans who eat infested pork, beef, or fish that has not been adequately cooked.

Cause: As many as six different types of tapeworm can live in the human digestive system, but the most common are fish, beef, and pork tapeworms. Tapeworms usually cause only mild symptoms, but beef and pork tapeworms occasionally produce more serious illnesses.

Incidence: Cases of human infestation with tapeworm are rare in the United States but common in Asia, eastern Europe, and Latin America. Beef and fish tapeworm are common in the United States, while pork tapeworm is most common in Latin America, Asia, and Europe.

Noticeable symptoms: Many people with tapeworm do not have symptoms. Those who do may feel abdominal pain or have diarrhea and excess gas. They may also experience nausea and vomiting. Other common symptoms include anal itching or inflammation. Hunger, fatigue, loss of appetite, and weight loss occur if the condition is not treated.

Phone doctor

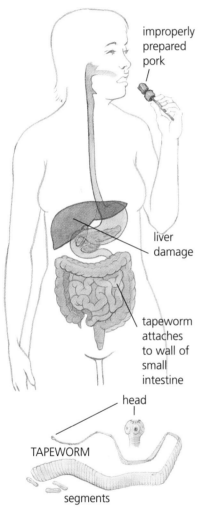

improperly prepared pork

liver damage

tapeworm attaches to wall of small intestine

head

TAPEWORM

segments

Tapeworm infestation
When a tapeworm infests a person, the worm lives in the intestines without causing much harm. But larvas of the worm may invade other parts of the body, including the brain, where cysts that result can be much more damaging.

In the rare situation in which larvas migrate to other organs of the body, including the brain, and form cysts, serious damage can result. This condition is called *cysticercosis* (SIHS-tih-suhr-KOH-sihs).

White, ribbonlike worm segments can sometimes be seen in the stool or on clothing or bedclothes. ***If you find a tapeworm segment, see a doctor and bring the segment with you.***

Diagnosis: A physician may take a stool sample or an anal scraping to detect worms or eggs.

Treatment options: The doctor may prescribe worm-killing medications if you have a tapeworm. Usually, a single dose is enough to eliminate the tapeworm.

Pernicious anemia can result from fish or beef tapeworm. To treat it, the physician may give you injections of vitamin B_{12}.

All cases of intestinal parasites require follow-up examinations to make sure that the treatment worked.

Stages and progress: Pigs, cattle, and fish become infested when they eat tapeworm eggs. The eggs hatch into potential tapeworms; these move into muscle where they form cysts, small structures that contain this stage of tapeworms. When humans eat raw or undercooked flesh that contains a cyst, the cyst passes into the intestines. Once in the small intestine, the cyst hatches, and a young tapeworm attaches to the intestinal wall. It absorbs food through the entire surface of its body. Tapeworms vary in length from less than an inch to more than 75 feet long, but most are less than 25 feet long. Some live in a person's body for more than 25 years.

Parts of the worm break off and are excreted in the stool. These parts contain eggs. Infestations may also be spread by food handlers, who may not even know that they have tapeworms, but humans are most often infested by the cysts, not the eggs.

Very large tapeworms can fill the diameter of the intestine, causing a blockage. Serious illness can result when beef tapeworm eggs are ingested. They hatch into larvas, are carried through the body in the bloodstream, and are deposited in muscle, brain, and other tissue, where they form cysts. Heavy infestation can cause serious damage.

Prevention and risk factors: Despite strict U.S. government

Wash hands

regulations, meat that contains tapeworm cysts occasionally gets on the market. Thoroughly cook fish, beef, and pork to destroy any cysts that may be present. Remember that any meat or fish served raw, such as steak tartare or sushi, may contain parasites. Wash your hands thoroughly with soap and warm water after using the toilet and before handling food.

When traveling abroad to areas where tapeworms are common, do not eat raw or undercooked beef, pork, or fish. If you become ill after traveling abroad, be sure to tell your physician where you have been.

Tay-Sachs disease
(TAY-saaks)

DISEASE

TYPE: GENETIC

See also
Gaucher disease
Genetic diseases

Tay-Sachs disease is a devastating inherited birth defect that belongs to a group known as *storage diseases*. An abnormal gene prevents body cells from producing an *enzyme,* or chemical facilitator, that normally helps break down specific chemical compounds. These compounds then get stored in cells, damaging or destroying them. In Tay-Sachs disease fatty molecules called lipids accumulate in cells of the central nervous system and gradually but inevitably stop them from working.

Cause: The enzyme deficiency is caused by a single recessive gene; that is, it must be inherited from both parents to have a noticeable effect.

Incidence: Like other storage diseases Tay-Sachs disease is generally uncommon. But it is highly concentrated in Ashkenazic Jews, originating in Central and Eastern Europe, and French Canadians, including the Louisiana Cajuns descended from them. In the United States about 1 in 27 Jews and Cajuns are carriers of the gene, compared with about 1 in 250 in the general population.

Noticeable symptoms: For about six months a newborn may seem perfectly normal, but then the infant stops smiling, crawling, or turning over. The hands are no longer able to reach out and grasp objects.

Diagnosis: At the age of about six months, a characteristic cherry-red spot can be observed with an ophthalmoscope in the back of each eye of an affected baby.

Blood tests can identify carrier parents and affected fetuses.

The level of the normal enzyme can be measured in parental blood or from fetal cells collected by amniocentesis or chorionic villi sampling (CVS). A fetus with the genetic defect will have no sign of the enzyme. An adult with an intermediate level of the enzyme is likely to be a carrier.

If the results of enzyme measurement are unclear, it is possible to identify specific mutations in the gene by DNA analysis. DNA analysis can also help identify much rarer forms of the condition that appear somewhat later in life but that have the same devastating consequences.

Treatment options: There is no cure and no treatment except keeping the child comfortable.

Outlook: Gradually, the baby becomes blind, paralyzed, and unresponsive. Essential life processes may continue for a while, but death usually occurs by age five.

T cells

See **Lymphocytes**

Teeth

BODY SYSTEM

See also
Dental illnesses and conditions
Digestive system
Gingivitis
Periodontal disease
Toothache
Tooth decay

The teeth and the bones are the hard tissues of the body. They get their strength and durability from the minerals—calcium and phosphorus—of which they are largely composed.

The first teeth to appear in the mouth are the 20 primary, or baby, teeth. These are pushed out and replaced during childhood and adolescence by the larger and stronger permanent teeth. By adulthood there will normally be 32 of these, 16 in each jaw.

Role: The main function of teeth is to break food into fragments small enough to swallow and digest. Human beings are omnivores—they eat both animal and vegetable food. Human teeth have two basic shapes to chew both kinds of food.

The front teeth—the chisel-shaped *incisors* and the pointed *canines*—perform the preliminary task of tearing and cutting food into pieces. The back teeth—the *molars*—have wide chewing surfaces to mash and grind the pieces that the front teeth have cut up. In between are intermediary teeth called *premolars;* these share characteristics with both front and back teeth.

Each of the front teeth has a single root. The back teeth,

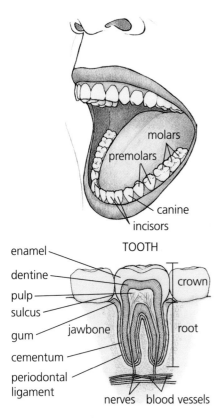

TOOTH

enamel
dentine
pulp
sulcus
gum — jawbone
cementum
periodontal
ligament

crown

root

nerves   blood vessels

Each of the matching pairs of upper and lower teeth has a specialized task in chopping up and grinding food. The tooth seen in detail is a molar, used for grinding.

which bear the heaviest pressures of chewing, have either two or three roots. The premolars have either one or two.

Anatomy of the tooth: A tooth has two main parts, the *crown* and the *root*. The crown is the part visible above the gum; it contains the biting surfaces. The root is the part normally located below the gum; it rests in a socket in the jawbone.

The crown has an outer layer of *enamel* that protects it from wear and decay. Enamel is made up almost entirely of calcium and phosphorus and is the hardest substance in the body. The less-exposed root is covered with a bonelike material called *cementum* (sih-MEHN-tuhm), thinner than enamel and not as hard.

Within these outer layers is the main structure of the tooth, the *dentin*. Dentin is less dense than enamel but somewhat denser than cementum. It contains numerous fine channels called *tubules* (TOO-byoolz) that radiate outward from the core of the tooth.

At the core is soft tissue called *pulp*. It occupies a hollow pulp chamber inside the crown and extends to the tip of each root through a slender root canal. The outermost part of the pulp is made up of cells called *odontoblasts* (oh-DON-tuh-BLAASTS); these have slender, threadlike extensions through the tubules in the dentin.

Conditions that affect the teeth: Besides the odontoblasts, the pulp is composed largely of blood vessels and sensory nerves. The blood vessels carry oxygen, minerals, and other substances to the odontoblasts and remove waste carbon dioxide. The nerves are sensitive to pressure, heat, cold, electricity, and chemicals such as acids. They may respond to these stimuli directly, but more often they respond indirectly when the odontoblasts are irritated.

The enamel and cementum have no sensation, and they normally shield the dentin and pulp from irritating stimuli. But if the shield becomes thin or damaged from tooth decay, wear, or the like, the odontoblasts may become exposed to such irritation and communicate it to the nerves. The nerves mainly respond by registering pain, ranging from mild tenderness (hypersensitivity) to toothache. If the damage penetrates to the pulp chamber itself, the pain may become severe.

When the teeth first erupt in childhood, the pulp is relatively large and close to the surface. As a result children's teeth tend to be more sensitive than those of adults. Later in life additional dentin forms inside the tooth, making the pulp chamber and root canals narrower. The teeth of older people become relatively insensitive. Eventually, the chamber and canals may fill in almost completely, so that very little pulp remains.

The roots of the teeth fit into sockets in the upper or lower jawbones. Part of each root extends out of the socket. This exposed root and the jawbone itself are covered and protected by the soft tissue of the gum. Where the gum meets the tooth at the base of the enamel, it forms a small cuff, which encloses a shallow, V-shaped hollow called a *sulcus* (SUL-kuhs). When plaque and calculus are allowed to collect in the sulcus, periodontal disease (periodontitis) is likely to result.

Temporal arteritis

(TEHM-puhr-uhl AHR-tuh-RIY-tihs)

DISEASE

TYPE: AUTOIMMUNE (?)

See also
Arteries
Autoimmune diseases
Eyes and vision
Headache
Immune system
Stroke

A sudden, persistent headache on one or both sides of the head may be the result of temporal arteritis, an inflammation of the branching temporal arteries in the temples on each side of the forehead (*tempora* is Latin for temples). The inflammation damages the arteries, thickening their walls and reducing the volume of blood they can carry.

Cause: Temporal arteritis is believed to be a localized form of a more general inflammatory disease of the arteries. Some experts suspect that it may be an autoimmune disease, in which the immune system produces antibodies not only against foreign invaders such as bacteria and viruses but also against the body's own cells, as if these too were foreign invaders. The autoimmune reaction inflames and damages the affected tissues.

Incidence: Temporal arteritis is largely confined to people over the age of 50, and the average age of onset is 70. Among those over 50, the disease occurs in about 2 in 1,000 persons. Women are more likely to be affected than men.

Noticeable symptoms: The characteristic pain is a throbbing ache rather like migraine, which comes on suddenly and becomes worse. It can be located in one or both temples. Under the skin the inflamed artery may be visibly red and

Emergency Room

swollen, and it may be tender to the touch. Other possible symptoms may include pain in the jaw when chewing, a low fever, loss of appetite and weight, and general weakness.

If one of the symptoms is impaired vision in one or both eyes, it should be considered an emergency that requires immediate medical attention.

Diagnosis: Definitive diagnosis may require a surgical biopsy of the artery to obtain a sample for microscopic examination. But in certain instances, particularly if impaired vision is a symptom, treatment may be advisable even before the diagnosis is confirmed.

Treatment options: Corticosteroid drugs, taken over an extended period, are used to halt the inflammation and keep it from returning. The chief danger is that nearby arteries serving the eyes may be involved, leading to blindness in one or both eyes.

Tendinitis

See **Tennis elbow and related problems; Torn or severed tendon**

Tennis elbow and related problems

INJURY

See also
Bursitis
Carpal tunnel syndrome
Fractures, dislocations, sprains, and strains
Muscles
Skeletal muscles
Torn or severed tendon

Tendons are straps of strong, fibrous connective tissue that attach muscles to bones. They do not themselves contract, but by firmly holding muscles and bones together, they help transform muscle contractions into movement.

Tendons are durable tissues that normally can withstand many years of use without problems developing. But sometimes they become torn or inflamed, producing pain and impairment. This condition is called *tendinitis* (TEHN-duh-NIY-tihs—"inflammation of the tendon").

Tendinitis generally occurs near the most heavily used joints of the body, those of the arms and legs. Its association with particular athletic activities gives it several popular names. When it occurs in the outer elbow, it is known as *tennis elbow* or more formally as *epicondylitis* (EHP-ih-KON-duh-LIY-tihs). When it occurs in the inner elbow, epicondylitis is *golfer's elbow.* When it occurs in the knee, it is known as *jumper's knee.* Other common locations include the shoulder and the Achilles tendon in the back of the ankle.

A closely related disorder is *tenosynovitis* (TEHN-oh-SIHN-uh-VIY-tihs), which often occurs in the fingers. Each tendon of the fingers is enclosed in a fluid-filled sheath, called a *synovial membrane,* through which the tendon slides smoothly back or forth as the finger opens or closes. If the sheath becomes inflamed, it also becomes constricted, making movement of the tendon through it stiff and painful. Tenosynovitis can also affect joints in the feet.

One of the typical effects of tenosynovitis is *trigger finger.* Fully opening a finger becomes difficult. First it resists, then suddenly gives way, often with an audible snap.

Cause: Tendinitis and tenosynovitis may be caused by a sudden wrench, the way a muscle sprain is. But usually they result from repeated minor strains over an extended period of time. Tenosynovitis of a finger is also sometimes caused by infection following a cut or other injury.

Incidence: Tendinitis is extremely common among people engaged in habitual heavy exertion of particular parts of the body. But since it usually results from long-repeated strains, it is most common among those of middle age or older. The same is true of tenosynovitis, unless it is caused by infection.

Noticeable symptoms: Tendinitis and tenosynovitis produce burning, stabbing pain that usually radiates from an area near a joint. Typically, the pain is aggravated by further exertion and relieved by rest.

Diagnosis: Although x-rays and blood tests are commonly taken, their purpose is to exclude other possible causes of distress since tendinitis does not show up on either but other causes do.

Treatment options: Tendinitis is treated like sprains, bursitis, or other inflammations of the region around the joints. The most important step is to prevent further irritation. Those who dismiss their pain or try to "play through" it generally just make their condition worse. Often, resting the inflamed tendon is enough to heal it, but sometimes a sling or splint must be used to immobilize it until the inflammation subsides.

Nonsteroidal anti-inflammatory drugs (NSAIDs) such as aspirin and ibuprofen can be used to relieve the pain and reduce inflammation. Applications of either heat or cold are more likely to be helpful. Alternating applications of heat with cold (contrast therapy) may be especially effective. As the injured tendon heals, massage and gentle exercise may help restore its normal function.

In severe cases injections of corticosteroids may provide quicker and more powerful relief than NSAIDS. But since corticosteroids can also cause permanent damage to the tissues, their use must be carefully limited and monitored.

Tenosynovitis is treated similarly to tendinitis. In some severe cases, however, surgery is needed to slit open the constricting sheath so that the tendon can move freely.

Tendinitis and tenosynovitis are almost always acute rather than chronic conditions. With proper care, recovery should eventually be complete.

Testes

(TEHS-teez)

BODY SYSTEM

See also
Elephantiasis
Endocrine system
Hernias
Impotence
Mumps
Penis
Prostate gland

The male glands known as the testes are also sometimes called the *testicles,* which is Latin for "little testes." The singular for testes is *testis.* The testes are the male reproductive glands, or *gonads,* corresponding to the ovaries in women.

Size and location: The testes are somewhat smaller than chicken eggs and roughly egg shaped. They are normally found in a pouch of skin beneath the base of the penis called the *scrotum* (SKROH-tuhm).

Role: The testes have two important products: the male hormone *testosterone* and *sperm.* Testosterone is an endocrine hormone released into the bloodstream. Sperm are produced in complex coiling passageways in the testes that combine to form a long (two-foot) tube called the *vas deferens* (VAAS DEHF-uhr-uhnz). The vas deferens carries the sperm back into the body, where they are gathered in an internal sac called the *seminal vesicle* (SEHM-uh-nuhl VEHS-ih-kuhl). The seminal vesicle contains a fluid that mixes with the sperm. When stimulated, the sperm and the fluid move through a tube called the *ejaculatory duct* past the *prostate gland,* which

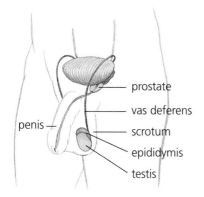

Temperature control
The testes are within the scrotum, outside the main body. This location is to produce a lower temperature, which is needed for proper formation of sperm.

Phone doctor

adds yet another fluid to the mixture. After this addition the combination is called *semen* (SEE-muhn). Semen is ejected into the birth canal during copulation.

The penis is so designed that urination and ejaculation cannot take place at the same time.

Conditions that affect the testes: Rarely, for one reason or another, a person is deprived of both testes in an act called *castration*. If a boy is castrated before puberty, he does not go through the changes of puberty.

Sometimes the testes remain inside a baby's body instead of moving into the scrotum. One undescended testis may not be a problem, although it can be corrected surgically and often is. Two undescended testes produce sterility because the temperature of the interior of the body is too high for sperm production.

If the place in the abdominal wall where the cord anchoring the testicles passes into the body is too large, a hernia may occur. Sometimes the hernia allows part of the intestines to descend into the scrotum, especially if the hernia existed at birth. If the anchoring cord becomes twisted or tangled (*testicular torsion*), it causes sudden swelling and considerable pain. This problem can only be resolved by surgery.

Cancer of the testes is rare, but can be detected in its early stages by self-examination for a lump. ***Any lump in a testis may be harmful and should be examined by a physician.*** The treatment is surgical removal of the testis. If done early, complications such as spread to the lungs can be avoided and recovery is complete. The other testis produces enough testosterone and sperm for normal living. Swelling of the entire testis is usually not harmful and often goes away by itself.

Some sexually transmitted diseases may invade the testes, causing pain and swelling; this is known as *orchitis* (awr-KIY-tihs). ***Any swelling of a testis should be examined by a physician.*** Injury and the mumps virus can also cause testicular swelling.

Production of the hormone testosterone tends to decline in older men, often resulting in muscle weakness. Sometimes lack of the hormone can produce or contribute to impotence.

Tetanus

(TEHT-n-uhs)

DISEASE

TYPE: INFECTIOUS
(BACTERIAL)

See also
Bacteria and disease
Convulsion
Meningitis
Muscles
Nerves
Poisoning
Spasm
Vaccination and disease

Phone doctor

Tetanus is a potentially life-threatening disease usually associated with infected puncture wounds; that is, deep wounds with a narrow opening. A typical first symptom of tetanus is stiffness and tightening of the jaw muscles, giving rise to the disease's other name, *lockjaw*. If tetanus is allowed to progress it brings on severe muscle spasms and full-blown muscle convulsions that can end in death.

Cause: A bacterium (*Clostridium tetani*) causes tetanus by producing a nerve toxin as it multiplies. The toxin causes spasms and convulsions or seizures by interfering with the nerves that control muscles. Tetanus bacteria commonly live in the intestines of animals—in the past horse manure was the main source of the bacteria. Infected feces contaminate the soil with bacterial spores. If such soil then gets deep beneath a break in the skin, the spores can grow into living bacteria and cause tetanus. The spores must be deep to be in a low-oxygen environment since the bacteria cannot survive in atmospheric oxygen. Therefore, contaminated punctures of the skin by wood splinters, nails, bullets, and even insect or animal bites are most likely to lead to tetanus.

Incidence and risk factors: In the United States tetanus has been reduced to about 50 cases a year, although it continues to be a major problem in developing nations.

Most tetanus cases in the United States occur in people who have not had recent vaccinations against the disease—a survey reported in 2002 shows that 72% of American adults have no immunity to tetanus.

Noticeable symptoms: Stiffness of jaw and neck muscles is usually the first symptom of tetanus. There will probably also be a slight fever, headache, chills, and irritability. Swallowing becomes difficult as well.

Any time you receive a wound you think might be infected with tetanus, seek prompt medical attention.

Diagnosis: Although the tightening of jaw muscles is a characteristic symptom of tetanus, some other diseases, including such central nervous system infections as meningitis, may cause it as well. Lockjaw can also be a symptom of strychnine poisoning.

Treatment options: All wounds should be washed, sterilized, and bandaged as soon as possible. The most important treatment for tetanus is prevention, however. If the patient has not been vaccinated for tetanus within the past five years, the doctor will administer a serum of antibodies to tetanus—tetanus immune globulin, or TIG—for immediate relief followed by a tetanus shot. Some authorities prefer to give a new tetanus vaccination instead of TIG. Because the toxin takes some time to build up in the system, vaccination can produce a surge of antibodies just when they are most likely to be needed.

If the tetanus has already reached an advanced stage when treatment begins, the patient becomes hypersensitive and must be kept in a quiet, dark room. Even minor noises, cold air drafts, or other mild irritants can stimulate seizures. Doctors can treat only the symptoms at this stage, giving the patient muscle relaxants, antibiotics, and sedatives. Oxygen administered under high pressure may also be useful, and the patient may need to be kept on a respirator for several weeks to maintain breathing.

Stages and progress: Typically, the first symptoms are felt eight to twelve days after infection, though sometimes they develop in as few as three days or in three weeks or more. As tetanus becomes more advanced, the muscles of the neck and face begin to spasm. Eventually, the back and abdominal muscles become involved. In severe infections it takes only a minor stimulus to set off a seizure. Breathing may become difficult or impossible during seizures of the respiratory muscles and, without medical intervention, death can result.

Tetanus shot

Prevention: Vaccination against tetanus prevents the disease for several years. Preferably, infants will get the first of five immunizing injections when they are about two months old. Their next shots should be given at four months, six months, eighteen months, and finally between four and six years of age. Adults should have their vaccinations renewed every ten years.

Effects on world population and health: Tetanus is one of the major health problems in developing countries. There it affects infants, who develop tetanus and die as a result of infection when their umbilical cords are cut under unsterile conditions. A campaign by the World Health Organization has reduced this *neonatal tetanus* from over 30,000 cases in the late 1980s to half that number by the twenty-first century.

Thalassemia

(THAAL-uh-SEE-mee-uh)

DISEASE

TYPE: GENETIC

See also
Anemias
Blood
Genetic diseases
Jaundice
Liver
Sickle cell anemia

Thalassemia refers to a group of hereditary blood diseases with very similar effects. Defects in the genes that control production of *hemoglobin,* the active molecule in red blood cells, prevent the normal transport of oxygen in the blood. The result is anemia, which produces such symptoms as weakness and breathlessness and which may lead to serious heart, bone, and liver damage, sometimes resulting in death from heart failure or infection.

There are two main types of thalassemia, and both share some of the characteristics of sickle cell anemia. Each is concentrated in parts of the world where malaria is common. *Beta thalassemia* (also known as *Cooley's anemia* or *Mediterranean anemia*) is concentrated among people who live around the Mediterranean Sea but is also found among people living in parts of Africa, India, and Pakistan. *Alpha thalassemia* is concentrated among the peoples of Southeast Asia.

Cause: The two forms of thalassemia are named for the two chains that make up the protein hemoglobin. In one form a gene for the alpha chain of hemoglobin is defective, while in the other it is the beta chain that is missing or nonfunctional. The serious forms of both diseases are recessive—the abnormal genes must be inherited from both parents. Children who inherit such genes from just one parent may have a mild, often unnoticeable form of the disease, often called *thalassemia minor.* But they also have something valuable, a natural resistance to malaria.

Incidence: Worldwide there may be as many as 100,000 persons who are severely affected, mostly children.

Noticeable symptoms: At birth babies may have no symptoms, but as their bodies produce more and more defective hemoglobin, the characteristic signs of anemia—paleness, weakness, and breathlessness—start to appear. There may also be jaundice. Those with thalassemia minor usually have no evident symptoms unless in a situation in which oxygen is scarce; then they may experience unusual fatigue.

Diagnosis: Most cases of the two diseases can be identified by blood tests. The specific gene defects involved can be identified, with some difficulty, by DNA analysis.

Treatment options: The standard treatment for either form of thalassemia is with frequent blood transfusions. These can lead to a dangerous buildup of iron in the body, so drugs called chelators must be used to help remove the excess iron in the system. A more experimental treatment that is permanent when successful is a bone-marrow transplant, since red blood cells are produced by the bone marrow.

Outlook: The outlook for both types of thalassemia is highly variable. Babies with the most serious form of alpha thalassemia are likely to be stillborn or to die in infancy. Those with serious beta thalassemia have an increasingly improved chance of survival but may nonetheless die relatively young.

Threadworm (strongyloidiasis)

(STRON-jih-loi-DIY-uh-sihs)

DISEASE

TYPE: PARASITIC

See also
Parasites and disease
Roundworms

Threadworm infection, or strongyloidiasis, is common in tropical and subtropical regions, where almost a quarter of the people may be infected. When threadworm infection is seen in people in temperate areas, such as most of the United States, the infection probably was obtained while the person was vacationing in a tropical area. The parasite is found in temperate parts of the eastern United States, however.

Cause: Theadworm infection in humans is caused by the tiny parasitic roundworm *Strongyloides stercoralis*, which lives in the soil. Infection occurs when the worm larvas burrow through the skin and into the bloodstream. This usually occurs when a person is walking barefoot.

Stages and progress: The threadworm travels through the circulatory system and enters the lungs. From there it is coughed up, then swallowed. The larvas stay in the intestines, where they mature into adult threadworms and lay eggs. The eggs hatch, and the new larvas leave the body with the feces. The adult worms can live in the intestines for up to five years, producing eggs.

The threadworm life cycle has a complicated course with various kinds of larvas. Larvas that develop in the intestine and are excreted are usually noninfectious. But in some individuals larvas of an infectious type are hatched while still within the body. These larvas can start the cycle of infection all over again.

Noticeable symptoms: The site of entry may look like a bug

Phone doctor

bite and be itchy—often very itchy. Infestation of the lungs is often without symptoms, but may cause coughing, breathing problems, or fever. Infestation of the intestines can result in diarrhea (sometimes bloody), cramps, nausea, and vomiting, depending on severity. ***Call a doctor whenever diarrhea lasts more than two or three days or is bloody.***

Diagnosis: A physician will do a blood test and take sputum and stool samples to look for the threadworms.

Treatment: In healthy people a short course of medicine usually cures the problem. Treatment is more difficult in people who are malnourished or have damaged immune systems.

Prevention: Good personal hygiene and wearing shoes outdoors are the most effective ways to prevent threadworm infection.

Thrombophlebitis

(THROM-boh-flih-BIY-tihs)

DISEASE

TYPE: MECHANICAL

See also
Arteries
Blood
Cancers
Circulatory system
Embolism
Inflammation
Varicose veins
Veins

Phlebitis is an inflammation of a vein, usually in the leg. When a blood clot, also called a *thrombus,* develops in an inflamed vein, the condition is called thrombophlebitis. Thrombophlebitis often affects veins close to the surface of the skin, but it may also occur in deep veins. Then it is referred to as *deep vein thrombosis.*

Cause: When a vein lining has been damaged, the body produces a clot. Blood platelets, the protein fibrin, and other blood components collect at the damaged area. These particles clump together into a solid mass—the clot. The clot may grow large enough to block the vein partially or even completely. The whole clot, or a piece of it, may break off and move to some other part of the body. If the clot lodges in a narrow part of an artery, blocking it, the block is called an embolism.

Superficial, or *surface, thrombophlebitis* is usually caused by a blow or injury to a leg or an arm, or by bacterial infection in a vein. When no other cause is apparent, surface thrombophlebitis can indicate cancer in the abdomen.

Deep vein thrombosis occurs when the vein lining has been damaged or when blood flow is sluggish. These conditions may result from prolonged bed rest during an illness or after an accident or surgery. In rare cases thrombophlebitis occurs in people who have an inherited tendency to develop blood clots.

Incidence and risk factors: Although it can affect people of any age, thrombophlebitis usually occurs in adults. It is slightly more common in women than in men. A person with varicose veins is particularly at risk, as is anyone with an arm or leg in a cast or who is immobile for an extended time, as when sitting still during a long car or plane trip. Other risk factors include obesity, pregnancy, cancer, smoking, oral contraceptives, or estrogen-replacement therapy.

Noticeable symptoms: If thrombophlebitis is superficial, there may be dull pain, heat, or itching in the affected area. That area may become red or swollen, and there may be a cordlike hardening along the affected vein.

When deep veins are involved, there may be no noticeable symptoms, but in other instances the leg becomes swollen and painful. The greatest danger is that a clot in the vein may move to the lungs, causing a *pulmonary embolism*. This is a serious condition and can be fatal. If the clot moves to the lungs, you may cough up blood, be short of breath, and feel chest pain. ***If you have these symptoms, seek emergency treatment.***

Emergency Room

Diagnosis: A physician will be able to detect surface vein thrombophlebitis by observation and the patient's reported symptoms. The doctor will also check to see if the affected area is painful when it is pressed.

If deep vein thrombosis is suspected, a Doppler ultrasound scan can be used for confirmation. Images created by ultrasound waves reveal obstructions or abnormal blood flow patterns.

Treatment options: If only the surface veins are affected, treatment will probably consist of application of warm moist compresses, elevation of the leg, and an anti-inflammatory painkiller such as ibuprofen. Properly treated, superficial thrombophlebitis usually clears up in one or two weeks.

If the deep veins are involved, the patient will have to stay in bed, probably in a hospital, until the pain and swelling are gone. Lying with the affected leg elevated higher than the heart and performing simple exercises such as wiggling toes and flexing leg muscles helps improve circulation. Anticoagulant medication such as aspirin, heparin, or warfarin will prevent further clot for-

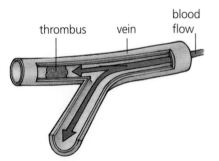

Thrombophlebitis starts when the inner wall of a vein is damaged. This produces a blood clot, or thrombus, that can break off and be carried to where it lodges in a narrow part of the vein, blocking blood flow.

mation. Clot-busting drugs such as streptokinase (STREHP-toh-KIHN-ays) or TPA may be injected into a vein to dissolve a clot that has already formed. Occasionally, a clot must be removed surgically.

The patient taking an anticoagulant may need to continue to do so for several months after leaving the hospital. Most patients continue to do exercises, especially walking, to improve blood circulation. Those with phlebitis of the leg also wear elastic support stockings throughout the day.

Prevention: Avoid prolonged standing or sitting. Women should not both smoke and take birth-control pills. If it is necessary to remain in bed for an extended period of time, ask the doctor if low doses of an anticoagulant are needed to prevent clots.

On long trips, wear comfortable clothes and shoes. Remove shoes while sitting. Stretch your legs, and do simple leg exercises in your seat. On a plane, bus, or train walk up and down the aisle at frequent intervals.

Thrombosis

See **Embolism**

Thrush

See **Candidiasis; Fungus diseases**

Thymus

BODY SYSTEM

The thymus is an important part of the immune system whose role was virtually unknown just a few decades ago. Like the spleen, the thymus is a large mass of lymphoid tissue that is more than just a large lymph node.

Size and location: The thymus is a medium-sized organ in the upper chest, just above the heart and below the thyroid. At its largest, around puberty, it weighs about an ounce. Adults, whose immune systems are more complete, need less work from the gland and it shrinks, almost disappearing in the elderly.

Role: The thymus looks as if it could be an endocrine gland (and was often identified as one in the past). It seems to be affected by the adrenal glands and the thyroid, which would support this interpretation. But it does not produce a hormone.

Instead, the main role for the thymus is formation of certain lymphocytes. These are the lymphocytes known as T cells (for *thymus cells*), one of the main parts of the immune system. Damage to T cells by HIV is the main cause of AIDS. If the thymus is removed from a very young animal, the animal fails to develop the immune response that causes transplant rejection, since T cells modulate this reaction. Such animals usually die long before maturity from infections because their immune system is compromised. Older animals, which have already developed a cadre of T cells, are generally unaffected by removal of the thymus.

Conditions that affect the thymus: The thymus seems to be involved in some way with the autoimmune disease myasthenia gravis, although the exact connection is unclear. In 10 to 15% of cases of myasthenia gravis, there is a tumor on the thymus. Sometimes removal of the thymus is used as a treatment for myasthenia gravis.

The thymus may suffer premature shrinkage as a result of starvation and is among the organs especially damaged by exposure to high levels of radiation.

Thyroid gland

(THIY-roid)

BODY SYSTEM

The thyroid gland regulates overall growth and the rate at which energy is used. The gland contains millions of tiny saclike structures that store a substance that can be converted into its major product, *thyroxine,* and into other chemicals. The thyroid is part of the body's endocrine system, glands that secrete hormones directly into the bloodstream.

Normal operation of the thyroid depends on the element iodine, an important component of thyroid hormones.

Size and location: Although the largest gland in the endocrine system the thyroid is no larger across than a golf ball. It wraps around the front of the windpipe, or trachea, in the neck. It rests just below the Adam's apple, or larynx.

Role: The thyroid controls various functions in the body by secreting hormones, mostly thyroxine. The overall rate of energy use, called metabolism, is mainly controlled by the thyroid. The hormones stimulate synthesis of protein, fat, and other substances and help regulate heart rhythms and the menstrual cycle. Some cells in the thyroid also secrete *calcitonin* (KAAL-sih-TOH-nihn), a hormone that plays a role in maintaining proper levels of calcium in the bloodstream.

The thyroid itself is regulated by the pituitary gland, which secretes thyroid-stimulating hormone (TSH). Increased levels of TSH in the blood cause the thyroid to secrete more thyroxine and other hormones.

Major malfunctions: Too little thyroid output, called *hypothyroidism*, produces the hormonal disorder *myxedema* (MIHK-sih-DEE-muh). Mild forms are characterized by patchy hair loss, dry skin, edema, and constipation. When thyroid levels are very low for long periods of time, deep apathy and depression develop.

In the United States hypothyroidism once was common in parts away from the oceans because of insufficient iodine in the diet—marine seafood is high in iodine. The lack of dietary iodine suppressed thyroid output and produced widespread goiter, a swelling of the thyroid gland. Introduction of iodized table salt has virtually eliminated hypothyroidism due to iodine deficiency.

A syndrome produced by prenatal or early childhood hypothyroidism is called *cretinism* (KREET-n-IHZ-uhm). Low thyroid activity retards growth and leads to developmental disability (mental retardation).

Too much thyroid output, called *hyperthyroidism* or *Graves' disease*, results in excess energy, with a heightened heart rate, higher metabolism, and weight loss. Its most serious symptom is bulging eyes, which can lead to vision loss. Graves' disease is an autoimmune disease; the thyroid is attacked by the immune system and responds by enlarging and producing more hormones.

Autoimmune attack is also the most common cause of hypothyroidism. In *Hashimoto's thyroiditis* the thyroid also swells, but eventually produces lower levels of hormone.

Thyroid cancer is uncommon and tends to grow slowly. However, thyroid cancer is a common result of exposure to radioactive iodine, a component in fallout from nuclear bombs or accidental releases from nuclear power plants. Cancer can be forestalled by taking pills containing nonradioactive iodine, which dilutes the radioactive type.

TIA (transient ischemic attack)

(ih-SKEE-mihk)

DISORDER

TYPE: MECHANICAL

See also
Atherosclerosis
Brain
Embolism
Hardening of the arteries
Hypertension
Stroke

Emergency Room

A transient ischemic attack, or TIA, is also known as a ministroke. It has the same symptoms as a stroke, but they are *transient*—they pass in a short time and cause no lasting damage. Like the most common form of stroke, a TIA is *ischemic*—caused by blockage of normal blood flow to the brain. And it is an attack—it begins suddenly and without warning and then disappears within a few minutes.

TIA is chiefly significant as a warning. About one in three individuals who have a TIA will never have another. Another one in three will experience at least one other TIA. And the last one in three will proceed to have a stroke, often within a year.

Cause: Like most cases of stroke TIA is caused by blood clots that block arteries or arterial branches delivering blood and nutrients to the brain. The difference is that in a TIA the blockage is temporary and ends before serious damage is done.

Incidence: TIA is probably even more common than stroke. Many instances go unrecorded.

Noticeable symptoms: The symptoms of TIA and stroke are the same, and there is no way to predict whether they signal a temporary, relatively harmless TIA or a potentially crippling or even fatal stroke. Thus, a person who experiences weakness, numbness, or paralysis; difficulty in speaking; dimmed, blurred vision; a sudden, very severe headache; or dizziness and loss of balance that last for perhaps ten or fifteen minutes is likely experiencing a TIA. ***If any of these symptoms occur, it is important to see a physician as soon as possible.***

Diagnosis: Imaging techniques, such as computed tomography (CT) and magnetic resonance imaging (MRI), can identify areas of damage in the brain. Ultrasound imaging or an arteriogram may be used to reveal narrowing or blockage in the carotid arteries serving the brain.

Treatment options: Platelet inhibitors such as aspirin and anticoagulant drugs such as warfarin may be prescribed to hinder the formation of blood clots. Cholesterol-reducing drugs may be used to help prevent the formation of plaques that may contribute to the formation of clots. In some cases surgery may be needed to open up carotid arteries and remove plaques from them.

Prevention: The best ways to prevent TIA from progressing to stroke are to control its risk factors.

- Obesity, high cholesterol, high blood pressure, and diabetes are best controlled by diet and exercise, supplemented by appropriate medications.
- Smoking, heavy drinking, and drug abuse may be ended by personal determination, but may require professional intervention as well.

Tic

SYMPTOM

See also
Diaphragm
Headache
Huntington's disease
Mental illnesses
Multiple sclerosis
Muscles
Nervous system
Spasm
Tourette's syndrome
Trigeminal neuralgia

A tic is an unintended twitch or spasm of some specific group of muscles that is repeated at irregular intervals and over irregular spans of time. Tics are one of the main forms of *movement disorder*. Transient tics may occur in as many as one out of seven children, much more often in boys than in girls.

Parts affected: Tics develop most often in the face and in the neck and shoulders, but may occur in any part of the body. Hiccupping represents a tic of the diaphragm in the respiratory system. The muscles that twitch in a tic are ones normally under voluntary control.

Related symptoms: *Tic douloureux* (TIHK DOO-luh-ROO) is a variety of tic consisting of spasms of intense pain on one side of the face. These pain spasms are accompanied by headaches.

Associations: Tics may begin in childhood as a result of head injuries or as a side effect of drugs. These often fade as a child grows older.

The disease Tourette's syndrome causes longer-lasting tics of the face, head, or shoulders, often accompanied by inappropriate sounds or words. Huntington's disease also has movement disorders as a primary symptom.

Tic douloureux is the principal symptom of trigeminal neuralgia. In rare cases it develops as a complication of multiple sclerosis.

Persons with severe mental illness who take antipsychotic medicines for a number of years may develop facial or bodily tics as a long-term side effect of those medicines. Those tics are part of the syndrome termed *tardive dyskinesia;* its symptoms often include tremors with or instead of tics.

Tinnitus

(tih-NIY-tuhs)

SYMPTOM

See also
Anemias
Cancers
Deafness
Heart failure
Labyrinthitis
Meniere's disease
Otitis media
Otosclerosis
Poisoning
Tumor, benign

Sometimes people complain that they hear a ringing in their ears that no one else can hear. This condition is called tinnitus. It is estimated that 7.9 million Americans experience it, three-quarters of them over the age of 45.

Parts affected: Tinnitus is usually a "ringing in the ears," although it can be a buzzing, roaring, whistling, or hissing that a person hears when there is no real sound present. It is accompanied by some hearing loss nine times out of ten.

Associations: Hearing loss may have any number of causes—exposure to loud sounds is thought to be the most common cause that also produces tinnitus. There may be an obstruction in the eustachian tube or in the outer ear canal due to a foreign object or buildup of earwax; an infection such as otitis media or labyrinthitis; or a chronic disease such as otosclerosis, Meniere's disease, cardiovascular disease, anemia, or the growth of tumors. Tinnitus may also be induced by injury to the head or reaction to certain drugs, alcohol, or pollutants such as carbon monoxide or heavy metals.

Prevention and possible actions: To prevent tinnitus, keep exposure to unnecessarily loud sounds to a minimum. Wear ear protection if it is necessary to work near planes or heavy machinery. Treat ear infections promptly.

Relief of symptoms: One theory is that partial deafness causes a person to hear a background sound that is always present but usually unnoticed. Many people with the condition play background music or other sounds to get relief from the constant sounds they hear because of tinnitus.

TMJ (temporomandibular joint dysfunction)

(TEHM-puh-roh-maan-DIHB-yuh-luhr)

DISORDER

TYPE: MECHANICAL

When the mouth opens and closes, only the lower jaw, the mandible, moves. It pivots and slides on joints at each end, joints that connect the mandible to the temporal bones of the cranium and so are called the temporomandibular joints (TMJs). The

See also
Dental illnesses and conditions
Pain
Teeth

movement of each joint is smoothed by a slippery, cushionlike disk of cartilage, which normally rests atop the end of the mandible.

Sometimes severe mechanical pressures of one kind or another cause the TMJs to malfunction. The cushioning disk may be pushed forward off the end of the mandible on one or both sides, and other soft tissues of the joint, such as ligaments and the enclosing capsule, may become painfully inflamed. This is *temporomandibular disorder (TMD),* known familiarly as TMJ.

Cause: Some TMJ pain may be caused by degenerative disease, such as rheumatic arthritis or osteoarthritis. Some TMJ inflammation and disk dislocation plainly result from trauma—whiplash injuries from motor vehicle accidents are often at fault. But a more common cause of TMD, in the view of many experts, is the habit called *bruxism*—grinding or clenching the teeth.

Noticeable symptoms: The main symptom is likely to be pain—but it may not be felt in the joints themselves. Headaches and neck pain are also common. A distinctive sign of disk dislocation is a clicking sensation that occurs when opening and shutting the jaw. It is caused by the shifting forward of the disk when the jaw opens and its return to the end of the mandible when the jaw closes. In many instances the dislocation is harmless, but sometimes it leads to inflammation and pain.

Diagnosis: Physical examination and the patient's own description of symptoms are often sufficient for diagnosis. Magnetic resonance imaging (MRI) can be used to image both the bones and soft tissues of the joint.

Treatment options: One standard form of treatment is a splint—a U-shaped piece of plastic that fits between the jaws and holds them slightly apart. Worn at night, it discourages bruxism and relieves pressure on the joints until the inflammation subsides.

Acute attacks are treated with anti-inflammatory painkillers such as aspirin and ibuprofen, muscle-relaxing drugs, physical therapy such as applications of heat or cold, and a soft diet to keep demands on the joint and chewing muscles to a minimum.

In very severe cases, when one or both joint disks are completely displaced, and opening the mouth is difficult or impossible, surgery may be effective in fastening the disk back in place or removing it completely.

No stress   Practice meditation

Prevention: It is generally agreed that one of the best ways to prevent TMD is to avoid or break the habit of bruxism, which can be controlled through stress management, such as relaxation exercises, meditation, or biofeedback.

Tobacco and disease

REFERENCE

Smoking is the inhaling and exhaling of fumes from burning tobacco, the habit of some 45 million Americans who puff on about 500 billion cigarettes a year. As a result one in five deaths in the United States is tobacco related—more than 400,000 deaths each year—making tobacco the leading cause of death, even ahead of obesity and lack of exercise. Worldwide the number is 4 million deaths annually.

Tobacco is also used without smoking. People chew it or sniff it in powdered form. These uses also affect health, causing cancer in parts of the body that directly touch tobacco and heart disease in the body as a whole. Chewing tobacco—also known as *smokeless tobacco*—increases the risk of oral cancer by four to seven times, depending on how heavily it is used.

Young people are particularly vulnerable to starting tobacco use because of peer pressure and because they are more easily impressed by advertising that glamorizes smoking. The Centers for Disease Control and Prevention reports that smoking rose among young people through 1997 but then began to decline slightly. The best advice offered to young people faced with making choices for themselves about becoming a smoker is "Don't start." Smoking tobacco is considered by experts to be more addictive than alcohol or illegal drugs.

What happens when people use tobacco: In the early decades of the twentieth century smoking was considered harmless. Americans consumed more than 1,000 cigarettes per person each year. But after World War II the American Cancer Society and other organizations started comparing death rates among smokers and nonsmokers. Then a government study concluded in 1964 that smoking is dangerous to health, and warnings to that effect were placed on cigarette packs.

One of the reasons for those warnings is that tobacco contains a naturally occurring addictive stimulant drug called *nicotine*. When smoking starts nicotine is carried to the brain in about seven seconds, where it activates a brain chemical called dopamine, bringing on a feeling of pleasure.

Tobacco smoke is a complicated mixture containing over 3,000 different substances, with at least 250 of them toxic or *carcinogenic* (KAHR-sihn-uh-JEHN-ihk)—able to cause cancer. The black tar from a burning cigarette is itself a carcinogen. Together nicotine and tobacco smoke are directly linked to the leading causes of death—heart attack and cancer.

Smoke in a confined area produced by persons smoking cigarettes, pipes, or cigars is called *second-hand smoke*. While this name implies that the smoke has been previously used, most second-hand smoke comes directly from the burning ends of cigarettes and cigars or from the pipe's bowl. This smoke contains more tars and nicotine than smoke that has been filtered,

Nicotine and tar
Because nicotine affects blood vessels, all parts of the body are damaged by tobacco use, but the main injury caused by nicotine is heart disease. Tar produces cancers of the respiratory system.

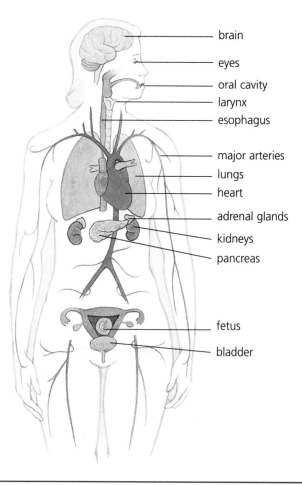

- brain
- eyes
- oral cavity
- larynx
- esophagus
- major arteries
- lungs
- heart
- adrenal glands
- kidneys
- pancreas
- fetus
- bladder

inhaled, and expelled. About 3,000 nonsmoking Americans die annually from lung cancer caused by second-hand smoke.

Diseases associated with smoking: The statistics that link tobacco with specific diseases are compelling. Long-term medical studies have found that overall death rates are twice as high among middle-aged men who smoke as those who do not. Listed below are some of the major diseases that have been linked to tobacco use in research studies.

Cardiovascular disease: More than a quarter of a million American deaths from cardiovascular disease are directly related to smoking, many more than from any other disease. In general there is a twofold increase in death from heart or coronary artery disease among smokers. Some cardiovascular diseases include heart attack, atherosclerosis, stroke, and angina pectoris. Cigarette smoking causes an increase of 50% in the chances of having a stroke. Among the other risks is *Buerger's disease*, which can lead to gangrene and loss of an extremity.

Nicotine also causes the adrenal glands to pump out epinephrine (adrenaline), which narrows blood vessels, makes the heart beat faster, and increases blood pressure. The amount of oxygen going to the heart is reduced.

Another component of cigarette smoke is carbon monoxide, the same gas that is an end product of incomplete combustion of gasoline. Carbon monoxide makes up 1 to 5% of cigarette smoke. When carbon monoxide is in contact with hemoglobin, the red pigment in blood, it binds to it tightly, preventing oxygen from binding with hemoglobin.

Inhaling another substance in tobacco, a glycoprotein, increases the clotting activity of the blood. This may injure blood vessel walls and lead to hardening of the arteries.

Cancer: Chief among cancers caused by tobacco is lung cancer, which makes up almost 30% of all U.S. cancer deaths. Lung cancer is seven times as likely to strike a smoker as a nonsmoker. Tobacco users have a fivefold increase in risk for cancer of the larynx, oral cavity, and esophagus. There is an increase of about one-third for cancers of the stomach, bladder, kidney, and pancreas.

Nearly 90% of all cases of lung cancer can be linked to smoking. Lung cancer kills over twice as many Americans as any other cancer.

Lung diseases other than cancer: Smokers have a fivefold increase in risk of dying from chronic bronchitis, emphysema, or chronic obstructive pulmonary disease (COPD). It makes asthma more dangerous and increases the risk of pneumonia.

Diseases affecting children: Mothers who smoke give birth to premature and underweight babies. Although many pregnant women realize how smoking can retard the growth of a fetus, some women resume smoking once the baby is born. Smoking in the same room as a baby gives an infant second-hand smoke. Nursing mothers or caregivers who smoke double or triple an infant's chances of dying of SIDS. Also, chronic respiratory illnesses are more common in nonsmoking children of smoking parents—the CDC estimates that nearly 300,000 children are affected this way.

Don't smoke

Quitting smoking

Almost 70% of the nation's 50 million or so smokers say that they want to quit, but the average smoker goes back three or four times before actually quitting for good. Nicotine creates a powerful addiction. People experience withdrawal symptoms, including irritability, lack of concentration, insomnia, tremors, sweating, severe coughing, and upset stomach when they try to quit.

The benefits of quitting can be life-saving. Within 20 minutes after the last inhalation of smoke, blood pressure drops down to normal. Within 8 to 48 hours carbon monoxide levels normalize. Over months lung tissue damage can be stabilized. Cardiovascular health returns to normal in about 3 years. Thus the risk of dying from a smoking-related disease goes down each year of not smoking.

People use various methods to quit. Gum, patches worn on the skin, and nasal sprays can provide small amounts of nicotine that are released into the body. In this way smokers taper off their need for nicotine over time. Use of this *nicotine replacement therapy* leads to greater success in quitting for good. Even with nicotine replacement, only one in four smokers stops smoking. About half the quitters remain smoke free. Drinking alcohol encourages relapses.

Tonsillitis
(TON-suh-LIY-tihs)

DISEASE

TYPE: INFECTIOUS

The tonsils are oval, walnut-sized masses of lymph tissue located at the back of the throat. In young children they collect organisms that invade the body through the mouth and alert the rest of the immune system to guard against them. But sometimes they become overwhelmed by the invading organisms. The infection, soreness, and swelling of the tonsils that follows is known as tonsillitis.

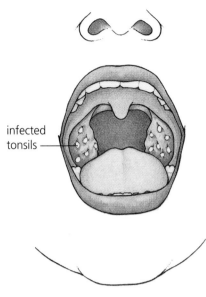

infected tonsils —

The tonsils are masses of lymphoid tissue at the back of the throat. When infected by bacteria, they often develop white spots as well as cause considerable throat pain.

Drink water

Avoid aspirin

Gargle saltwater

Phone doctor

See also
Bacteria and disease
Kidney diseases
Scarlet fever
Sore throat
"Strep"

Cause: Tonsillitis can be caused by any number of bacterial or viral organisms, but the most serious is the *Streptococcus* bacterium that also causes "strep" throat.

Incidence: Almost every child experiences a bout or two with tonsillitis. Even those youngsters who suffer tonsillitis frequently begin to have fewer instances after age seven, however, because their systems develop greater resistance to the germs that cause it.

Noticeable symptoms: A slight sore throat may be the only symptom, but a severe case inflames and swells the tonsils. It usually is accompanied by severe sore throat and high fever.

Diagnosis: In severe cases a doctor will take a throat culture to determine if strep throat has caused the tonsillitis to flare up. A special kit for the doctor's office can be used to quickly determine if the bacteria involved is *Streptococcus*.

Treatment options: If the swelling and sore throat associated with the tonsillitis are mild, the patient should rest and drink plenty of liquids. Gargling with a solution of warm water and salt will help the sore throat. *If the child is 16 or younger, do not give aspirin. Use acetaminophen if pain relief is needed.*

Get medical attention for tonsillitis that does not improve after 48 hours. If strep bacteria are involved, the doctor will probably prescribe oral antibiotics.

Stages and progress: While mild cases of tonsillitis generally clear up within two days, more severe cases can persist.

Before antibiotics became available, tonsillitis infections sometimes led to the heart disease rheumatic fever or the kidney disease nephritis. If a doctor prescribes antibiotics, it is especially important to continue taking them for the full term, not just until symptoms disappear. That prevents the infection from developing into rheumatic fever or nephritis.

Prevention: Though most children who have frequent attacks of tonsillitis outgrow this disorder as the tonsils shrink after the age of five, a doctor sometimes recommends surgery to remove the tonsils—usually when swollen tonsils interfere with the child's breathing or repeated infections affect the child's general

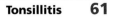

health. Sometimes other small masses of lymphoid tissue, the *adenoids* (AAD-n-oidz), also interfere with breathing and are removed as well.

Toothache

SYMPTOM

See also
Abscess
Dental illnesses and conditions
Endocarditis
Sinusitis
Teeth
Tooth decay

Nearly every older person has experienced the pain of a toothache at one time or another. The most common cause of toothache is tooth decay, but it may also result from other tooth damage, such as fracture or severe wear. With improvements in dental care Americans who are young today may live a long time without knowing toothache.

Parts affected: The outer layers of a tooth, its enamel and dentin, are mainly composed of minerals, which have no feeling. The sensory nerves are confined to the soft pulp of the tooth, located in a pulp chamber inside the crown and in root canals that extend to the tip of each root. These sensory nerves, especially those that register pain, react strongly to direct or indirect irritation of the pulp. The result is toothache.

The pain of toothache can be intense. One reason is that irritation of the pulp is also likely to cause inflammation. Inflamed tissue naturally swells, but inflamed pulp is restricted from swelling by the surrounding hard tissue of the tooth. The added pressure stimulates the pain-sensing nerves further and makes the pain worse.

Related symptoms: Tooth decay can allow bacteria to spread to the end of the tooth. There the bacteria form a painful abscess, which may require removing the nerves, effectively killing the tooth (*root canal*) as part of the treatment.

Associations: If bacteria from an infected tooth get into the bloodstream, they can infect the sinuses and cause sinusitis or, more dangerously, the heart valves to produce endocarditis.

Relief of symptoms: Toothache can be somewhat relieved by painkillers such as aspirin and ibuprofen and by applications of ice. If the pain is caused by tooth decay, heat is not recommended; it encourages the growth of bacteria and makes the condition worse. The only way to remedy the symptom completely is dental treatment to remove its cause.

Tooth decay

Teeth are among the densest, hardest tissues of the body. The enamel on their crowns is the hardest substance of all, and it can endure many years of wear from chewing. But for all their strength, teeth will, under certain conditions, decay.

Cause: There are three necessary conditions for tooth decay:

- *Bacteria.* The warm, wet interior of the mouth is a welcoming environment for bacteria, and there is no way of getting rid of them entirely. Antiseptic mouthwashes and brushing may reduce their numbers, but the effect is only temporary.
- *Sugar.* Bacteria need food to survive. The bacteria that cause tooth decay need sugar in some form. The modern diet is rich in sugar, and tooth decay is described as a "disease of civilization."
- *Teeth (and tooth surfaces) susceptible to decay.* Some people inherit teeth that are especially vulnerable to decay. The teeth of children and adolescents tend to be more susceptible than those of adults. In later life the teeth again become more susceptible as the gums naturally recede from the enamel crowns and expose the softer *cementum*—a bone-like material—around the roots.

Certain kinds of tooth surfaces are especially likely to be attacked: the grooves on top of the molars and premolars, the surfaces between adjacent teeth, the gumlines where the teeth meet the gums, and the leaky margins of old fillings.

When food debris and bacteria are allowed to remain undisturbed on the teeth for more than a day or so, they form a sticky film called *plaque.* As the bacteria digest sugar, they release acids; plaque holds these acids firmly against the teeth. The acids then dissolve the minerals in the teeth. The result is tooth decay, starting at the surface of the tooth and gradually penetrating inward.

Incidence: Tooth decay, to one extent or another, is almost universal. It occurs less in societies where little sugar is eaten. It is also less prevalent among people who receive modern dental care from infancy on. Yet by old age there are few people anywhere who escape it completely.

Noticeable symptoms: Tooth decay in its early stages is invisible and produces no symptoms. Only when it is well advanced does it cause any sensitivity or pain.

Diagnosis: Even at its earliest stages a dentist can often identify tooth decay during a routine examination using the pointed instrument called a dental explorer supplemented by x-rays that show decay as a small shadow of reduced density.

Treatment options: Most tooth decay can be successfully treated and need not result in the extraction of the tooth. The kind of treatment depends on the severity of the decay.

Filling: Drilling out the decayed matter and replacing it with an inert material called a filling is the simplest and most common way of treating a cavity. This approach is appropriate for relatively mild cavities, which are limited to the outer coat of enamel and the hard inner *dentin* and do not reach the *pulp*, the soft core where the nerves reside. Modern anesthetics make the process painless.

Several different materials are available for fillings. Amalgam, a mixture of mercury, silver, and other metals, is the most familiar. Gold is more durable than amalgam, so it is sometimes used on areas that get a lot of wear and pressure, such as the high points, or cusps, of the molars. Tooth-colored materials, such as composites, do not have the strength of metal but are often used on clearly visible front teeth. Ceramic fillings, usually porcelain, are used in the same way and last longer, but they require more time and skill to install and are more expensive.

Root canal therapy: When decay has penetrated so far that the pulp is severely infected, damaged, or dead, root canal therapy may be the only way to save the tooth. The pulp is completely removed, down to the tip of each root canal. The empty cavity is then partly filled with a natural resin called *gutta percha* and sealed with a filling. Sometimes the tooth is so weakened that its outer enamel must be ground off and replaced with an artificial crown of metal or porcelain.

Stages: Tooth decay proceeds in a series of distinct stages:

Decay of enamel: The first stage is the dissolving of the enamel. Decay usually starts with a tiny pit on the surface, which enlarges to form a cone-shaped "soft spot" underneath.

But since enamel is made up almost entirely of minerals and contains no living cells, this stage of decay is usually painless.

Penetration of dentin: If decay of the enamel is not treated, it is likely to penetrate the underlying dentin. Dentin is less dense than enamel, and decay spreads faster there. It is likely to form a second, soft cone of disintegrated material under the enamel. Even if there is sound enamel over the decayed dentin, it becomes undermined and likely to collapse. At this stage the damage may become an easily observed hole—a cavity.

Dentin is made up partly of minerals, but it also has narrow tubular channels that contain slender extensions of cells of the outer pulp called *odontoblasts.* Decay damages both. Acids dissolve the minerals, and bacteria infect the odontoblasts. The inflamed odontoblasts may in turn stimulate the sensory nerves deeper in the pulp. So this is the stage when decay may first be sensed. The tooth may become unusually sensitive to heat, cold, or pressure, or it may actually start to ache. Often, though, even severe decay of the dentin produces no noticeable symptoms.

Penetration of pulp: If decay reaches the pulp of the tooth, which contains the nerves and blood vessels, the tooth is very likely to ache. The inflamed soft tissue tries to swell but is restricted by the hard tissue around it, so the pain may become intense. Even at this stage, however, there may be no symptoms.

The survival of the tooth is now in danger. The pulp may become infected by bacteria, and the inflammation and infection may spread from the tip of the root canal to the bone of the tooth socket, forming an inflamed hollow, or abscess. Bacteria may be carried in the blood to other parts of the body as well. Infection may cause the soft tissues of the face to swell, a condition called *cellulitis* (SEHL-yuh-LIY-tihs).

Prevention: Brushing and flossing the teeth at least once every 24 hours are necessary to prevent the buildup of the plaque that directly leads to decay. Limiting sugar in the diet can also be helpful, especially for small children, but it can be difficult to carry out. Antiseptic rinses and chewing gum that contains a chemical compound called xylitol may provide at least temporary reduction of the level of bacteria in the mouth.

Among the best weapons against decay are fluorides—chemical compounds that contain fluorine. They are most

Thorough brushing after meals is among the most important ways to prevent tooth decay. Electric toothbrushes can remove plaque better than the most vigorous manual brushing.

effective when taken internally during infancy and childhood in the form of fluoridated water, drops, or tablets. They strengthen the tooth enamel while it is still developing. After the teeth have erupted, topical application of fluorides, in fluoride toothpaste or fluoride rinses, gives additional protection. The widespread use of fluorides has greatly reduced the incidence of tooth decay in the United States.

When the permanent molars and premolars erupt, the hard-to-clean grooves in their surfaces can be further protected with sealants. Sealants are long-lasting coatings of transparent plastic painted on the chewing surfaces.

Torn meniscus

(muh-NIHS-kuhs)

INJURY

See also
Cartilage
Ligaments
Skeleton

Phone doctor

A meniscus is a crescent-shaped wafer of cartilage in the knee. A torn meniscus can be very painful and may limit movement of the knee joint.

Parts affected: Each knee has two meniscuses: one on the inside (medial meniscus), another on the outside (lateral meniscus). The main function of the meniscuses, which are held in position by ligaments, is to act as shock absorbers, cushioning the point where the upper and lower leg bones meet. When a meniscus tears, protection is reduced. Pieces of the meniscus float in the joint and can become stuck between the leg bones, causing deterioration and pain.

Cause: Common causes include accidents, carrying heavy loads over long periods of time, sports activities in which a foot stays in one place while the upper leg twists, and deterioration due to aging. In minor tears the meniscus remains connected to the knee. In major tears it becomes almost completely unattached.

Noticeable symptoms: The most common symptom of a torn meniscus is sharp pain, especially when the knee is held straight or while twisting or squatting. Many patients also experience swelling in the knee and a loss of joint mobility. Sometimes the knee locks or temporarily gets stuck in one position. Untreated, the torn meniscus may damage a joint permanently. If a knee swells after twisting it, see a physician for an evaluation.

Diagnosis: A physician physically examines the knee to determine the site of the pain. An MRI scan is used to produce images of the knee to show the amount of damage. Arthroscopy may be performed. In this procedure a lighted surgical instrument called an arthroscope is inserted into the joint through a small incision. Images of the joint's interior are then projected onto a screen for diagnosis.

Treatment options: Treatment depends on the extent of the injury and the patient's age and general health. Treatment often includes surgery and a regimen of muscle-strengthening exercises. Ice packs and over-the-counter pain medications may help reduce pain. Heat may combat stiffness. Activities that increase knee pain should be avoided.

Torn or severed tendon

INJURY

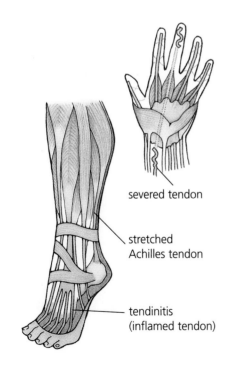

severed tendon

stretched Achilles tendon

tendinitis (inflamed tendon)

Tendons are the tough cords that connect the muscles to the bones they move. A torn or severed tendon is a serious injury that requires immediate medical attention. Depending on which tendon has been cut or torn, a person may lose the ability to move a finger, a toe, or even the whole foot.

Cause: Though tendons are made of very tough fibrous material, they can be cut. In an automobile accident, for example, a piece of sharp metal or broken glass may sever a tendon. A person can tear a tendon while jumping, during an accidental fall, or while engaging in strenuous physical exertion, as in sports. Less serious damage to the tendon may result in an inflammation called *tendinitis,* usually the result of long overuse rather than a single movement.

Sometimes a muscle tears instead of a tendon. Torn muscles are treated in much the same way as torn tendons, with a similar outlook for successful recovery.

Incidence: The Achilles tendon, the tendon that runs down the back of the ankle, is the one most frequently torn by physical exertion or accidental falls. Torn finger tendons, knee tendons, and Achilles tendons are fairly common complications in rheumatoid arthritis.

The tendons are subject to inflammation, stretching, tearing, and being cut or severed.

Emergency Room

See also
Fractures, dislocations, sprains, and strains
Skeletal muscles
Tennis elbow and related problems
Torn meniscus

Noticeable symptoms: There will be sudden pain and perhaps also a snapping sound at the time of injury. After a tendon is cut or torn, the victim cannot move the affected finger, toe, or other part. If the Achilles tendon is torn, the victim will be unable to move the ankle, and the back of the ankle will become swollen. ***See a doctor or go to a hospital emergency room as soon as possible after cutting or tearing a tendon.***

Treatment options: The torn or severed ends of a tendon tend to snap away from each other because they are normally under considerable tension. In order to reattach the two ends, a surgeon must make a long incision, find the two ends, and pull them back together. Once the ends have been refastened, complete recovery is usually ensured. In some cases, however, there may be some stiffness or reduced range of motion in the finger or other part involved.

Tourette's syndrome

(too-REHTS)

DISEASE

TYPE: GENETIC

See also
ADHD (attention-deficit/ hyperactivity disorder)
Genetic diseases
Tic

Tourette's syndrome (TS), named for Gilles de la Tourette, who described it in the late 1800s, is characterized by uncontrolled muscle movements, or tics, that can cause repetitive motions and vocal outbursts.

Cause: TS is inherited as a dominant gene. It is thought that neurotransmitters, chemicals used by nerve cells to communicate with one another, play a role in TS. Although the movements may seem similar to behavior categorized as obsessive-compulsive, many experts feel that the two diseases are not comparable. People with obsessive-compulsive behavior feel that something terrible will happen if they do not complete a behavior. People with TS describe their tics as trying to stop a sneeze—they can do so if they wish, but it is more comfortable to let the tics happen.

Symptoms usually begin in childhood or early adolescence, are most pronounced in the teen years, then lessen as the person gets older. Tourette's syndrome can be severe or so mild that it is not recognized.

Incidence: It was once thought that Tourette's syndrome was very rare—and the severe form is—but it is now estimated that at least 1 of every 200 people in the United States has some form of TS. Although it is not inherited as a sex-linked gene, males are four times more likely to experience TS than females. Symptoms normally start before age 21.

Noticeable symptoms: TS usually begins with facial tics such as eye blinking, nose twitching, or grimacing. Those symptoms may progress to more complex muscle tics such as neck craning, head jerking, bending and twisting, foot stamping, and involuntary vocal outbursts. Vocalizations may be profane or include other inappropriate language, but they can also be clearing of the throat, coughing, barking, or grunting.

Diagnosis: A diagnosis of Tourette's syndrome requires that the symptoms occur for at least one year and include both muscle tics and vocalizations. A thorough family history is also essential because this is an inherited disease. Often a doctor will do a battery of tests to rule out other conditions.

Treatment: There are no medications specifically for Tourette's syndrome, but some are used to target severe symptoms. As symptoms change or become more or less severe, medications may need to be changed to be effective. The medications used to treat the symptoms often have serious side effects, so it is necessary to balance the dosage for the patient to get the greatest benefit with the fewest side effects.

Controlling the symptoms of TS is very important in people with severe cases since the tics can prevent them from having normal lives. But medication is usually not prescribed for people with mild TS symptoms or infrequent symptoms. Those individuals can live normal lives, so the risks of the medications outweigh the small benefits that might ensue.

Outlook: Tourette's syndrome becomes less severe in most people as they mature. Although TS is a lifelong and chronic condition, most people with it can live a normal life and have a normal lifespan.

For many people with TS the severity of their symptoms ebbs and flows. They may even go for months with no tics or vocalizations at all. This is especially true in adulthood. There is some evidence that the severity of symptoms is related to stress and other environmental factors. By identifying those individual factors and controlling them, people with TS may gain some control over their symptoms.

Toxic shock syndrome

DISEASE

TYPE: INFECTIOUS
      (BACTERIAL)

See also
Bacteria and disease
Blood poisoning
Fever
Kidney diseases
Shock
"Staph"

In the 1980s there was an epidemic of severe illness and sudden death from an unknown cause among young women. Doctors found that the women got sick soon after their menstrual periods began and that most used tampons.

Cause: Toxic shock syndrome (TSS) occurs when bacteria multiply in the body and release poisons into the bloodstream. The poison, or toxin, causes a series of changes in the body that lead to shock. Several bacteria can cause TSS, but *Staphylococcus aureus* is the bacterium most people associate with it.

The tampons with synthetic fibers that were related to TSS are no longer on the market. Newer tampons include varieties made totally of cotton fibers, but studies have not shown these to be any safer. Women who are sensitive to the toxins can become ill if the tampons are not changed often enough—at least every six to eight hours. Using a diaphragm for birth control, recent childbirth, and recent nasal surgery are also associated with TSS.

Wounds infected with "staph" bacteria can also produce toxic shock. The same kind of infection is more often associated with blood poisoning, but it is thought that certain strains of staph produce more virulent poisons that induce shock.

Incidence: Although TSS is associated with young women, it can occur in older women, men, and children. *Staphylococcus aureus* is normally found on the skin and other parts of the body. Under the right conditions anyone with an open wound could be affected by the toxins. Fortunately, TSS is rare. In 1989 there were 400 cases in the United States; by 1996 there were only about 100 cases each year. About 1 in 20 cases is fatal.

Noticeable symptoms: TSS causes a beet-red rash, chills, fever (102°F or higher), headache, and vomiting or diarrhea. The symptoms come on quickly. The blood pressure falls, and the person goes into shock. In shock extremely low blood pressure can deprive vital organs of enough blood to function correctly; the lungs, kidneys, and liver are especially vulnerable. *If you have symptoms of toxic shock, especially when wearing a tampon or diaphragm, after surgery, or after harboring a festering wound, seek emergency medical assistance immediately.*

Emergency Room

Diagnosis: Blood pressure will be very low, and the white blood cell count will be high, indicating an infection. If a woman is within five days of the beginning of her menstrual flow and has been using high-absorbency tampons, TSS should be considered. It is important to tell a doctor about tampon use so that treatment of the shock can begin immediately.

Treatment options: Shock requires hospitalization, possibly in an intensive care unit. Intravenous fluid treatment is given to replace fluids lost because of the high fever and to increase the amount of fluid in the bloodstream; this raises the low blood pressure. The infection is treated with antibiotics. Close medical attention is needed until the infection is under control, the fever is down, the blood pressure is back up to normal, and all body organs are functioning properly.

Stages and progress: TSS is not fully understood. It appears that the bacteria grow and reproduce in a favorable environment, such as a tampon or a wound. Here they produce toxins. Different people have different sensitivities to these toxins. In those who are very sensitive to the toxins, the symptoms come on suddenly and pose an immediate health threat. People with less sensitivity may still be affected and become ill, but with milder symptoms.

Prevention: Most women should alternate tampons with sanitary napkins during menstrual periods. Women who have had TSS have a 30% chance of having it again, so should not use tampons.

Toxoplasmosis
(TOK-soh-plaaz-MOH-sihs)

DISEASE

TYPE: INFECTIOUS
(PARASITIC)

Toxoplasmosis is a very common infection. Part of its life cycle must take place in the intestines of a cat.

A woman who becomes infected during pregnancy runs a risk of infecting her fetus, with potentially disastrous results. Fetal infection may be quickly fatal, causing miscarriage, stillbirth, or death in early infancy. About one in ten infected babies are born with obvious symptoms of the disease.

The rest show no such signs and are likely to go undiagnosed. These infected infants are at high risk of serious health problems months or even years later. The parasites remain active and can eventually cause developmental disability (mental retardation), epilepsy, cerebral palsy, hearing loss, or impaired vision.

Cause: A parasitic one-celled protozoan causes toxoplasmosis. Infection with this parasite tends to occur either from eating raw or rare meat from infected animals, particularly sheep or pigs, or through contact with the feces of an infected cat. Cat feces often contain long-lived eggs of the parasite; these can be picked up accidentally in handling cat litter or touching contaminated soil.

Incidence: Toxoplasmosis triggers the body's immune system to develop antibodies to the parasite that causes it, giving permanent immunity after infection. About 85% of American women of childbearing age have never been infected and so have no immunity to the disease. Those who become infected during pregnancy have a 40% chance of infecting the fetus; the earlier in the pregnancy that the infection occurs, the more serious the consequences. Somewhere between 1 in 1,000 and 1 in 10,000 babies are born infected.

Noticeable symptoms: The infection usually produces only vague, flulike symptoms, such as slightly swollen glands or a low fever in an adult. Only those people with severely damaged immune systems become more seriously ill.

An infected newborn baby may suffer from jaundice, eye disorders, an evidently enlarged liver, or pneumonia. Most, however, have no noticeable symptoms. Eye inflammation remains a common symptom of continued infection.

Diagnosis: Antibodies that indicate earlier infection can be readily identified by a blood test. If a pregnant woman is discovered to be actively infected, it is possible through such tests as amniocentesis to determine whether the fetus is infected. Toxoplasmosis can also be diagnosed in newborn babies.

Treatment options: If a pregnant woman is infected but the fetus is not, the antibiotic spiramycin can substantially reduce the risk of transmission. If the fetus is infected, giving the mother the drugs pyrimethamine and sulfadiazine reduces the risk of adverse consequences in the baby. Following birth, treating the baby with the same drugs renders the parasites inactive in most cases.

Prevention: During pregnancy a woman who is not immune to toxoplasmosis should take the following precautions:

Avoid ingesting raw or rare meat, especially lamb and pork.

- In the kitchen wear disposable gloves when handling raw meat and wash your hands thoroughly afterward.
- Carefully clean kitchen utensils and surfaces used in the preparation and cooking of meat.

Reduce the risk of your cat's becoming infected.

- Keep your cat indoors to keep it from hunting or from picking up parasite eggs on its paws.
- Do not feed your cat raw or undercooked meat.

Avoid contact with cat feces.

- Change litter every day, before the excreted eggs can become infectious.
- Have someone else clean the litter box, or at least wear disposable gloves.
- Do not garden without gloves or go barefoot outdoors.
- Avoid outdoor sandboxes, often used by cats for excretion.

A woman who chooses to be tested before she becomes pregnant can find out if she is susceptible to infection or already immune. She can then be tested again during pregnancy to find out if she has recently been infected. Active infection can also be confirmed by other blood tests.

Trachea

(TRAY-kee-uh)

BODY SYSTEM

The trachea is a hollow tube that helps conduct air to and from the lungs. Also called the *windpipe,* it is attached to the larynx at the upper end. Two smaller air passages, the bronchial tubes, split off from its lower end and feed the air to the lungs.

Size and location: A bit more than half an inch wide and about four inches long, the trachea is located in the middle of the upper chest. It lies in front of the esophagus and is reinforced by stiff, U-shaped pieces of cartilage.

Role: The trachea channels fresh air into the lungs as a person breathes in. Then, as a person breathes out, the trachea carries the exhaled air from the lungs back up to the throat. It also filters out small particles of dust and other foreign material that may be in the air. The particles become trapped on the sticky mucous membrane lining the inside of the trachea. Then the many small hairlike structures (*cilia*) growing out of this membrane gradually move the mucous and foreign particles up the trachea to the throat. Muscles contract to narrow the trachea during coughing; this helps remove foreign particles lodged there.

Conditions that affect the trachea: People sometimes have a piece of food or other foreign object stick in the windpipe. If the obstruction completely blocks the flow of air, the person may die from lack of air (asphyxia) without emergency first aid. (See the description in Volume 1, page 72, of this set of how to perform the Heimlich maneuver to clear the trachea.)

Physicians sometimes perform a *tracheotomy* (TRAY-kee-OT-uh-mee) to remove foreign objects stuck in the trachea or to open the airway in an emergency. This involves making a small incision into the lower part of the patient's neck, creating a small opening into the trachea. A *tracheostomy* is surgery that creates a complete opening. It may be done to allow a patient to keep breathing despite a severely swollen throat or a physical injury to the upper airway.

Other conditions affecting the trachea include infections, such as bronchitis, and benign and cancerous tumors. Young children may stop breathing when *tracheitis* from bacterial infection closes the windpipe; a tracheostomy is required until the inflammation subsides.

Trachoma
(truh-KOH-muh)

DISEASE

TYPE: INFECTIOUS (BACTERIAL)

Trachoma, the world's most common cause of blindness, is highly contagious.

Cause: Trachoma is caused by the bacterium *Chlamydia trachomatis*. It is very contagious, particularly during early stages of the disease. Trachoma is transmitted from one person to another through contaminated fingers, towels, eye cosmetics, and so on. Flies may also transmit the disease.

Incidence: Trachoma affects as many as 500 million people around the world, mainly in poor rural areas where people live in overcrowded conditions and have limited access to water and sanitation.

Noticeable symptoms: Early signs of trachoma include pink eye (conjunctivitis), watering of the eyes, swollen eyelids, and sensitivity to light. Small lumps called follicles develop in the tissue that lines the upper eyelid. It is important to see a doctor if these symptoms appear.

Phone doctor

Diagnosis: A sample of tissue from the eyelid will be taken and examined for the presence of *Chlamydia trachomatis*.

Treatment options: The physician will prescribe antibiotics, which may include both oral medication and an ointment applied to the eyes. In advanced cases, when there is scarring of the cornea, surgery may be necessary.

See also
Bacteria and disease
Eyes and vision
Pink eye

Stages and progress: Following infection there is an incubation period of about one week before the first symptoms appear. Another week passes before the first follicles appear. Over a period of several weeks there is an increase in the number and size of these follicles. Gradually, an abnormal membrane begins to grow from the tissue lining the eyelid, covering the cornea. This leads to loss of vision. As the inside of the upper eyelid becomes roughened with scar tissue, it rolls inward and the eyelashes rub against the cornea. Ulcers, or sores, develop in the cornea, opening the way to new bacterial infections and additional loss of vision.

Wash hands

Prevention: Careful washing of hands and other measures of good hygiene can help prevent the spread of this disease. Dosing entire villages with antibiotics has been effective in sharply reducing infection rates in parts of Africa.

Trench mouth

DISEASE

TYPE: INFECTIOUS
(BACTERIAL)

Trench mouth got its name during World War I when it was a common ailment among soldiers in the front lines. It is an inflammatory disease of the edges of the gums, especially in the areas between the teeth. It tends to appear suddenly and come back periodically.

Trench mouth is also called *Vincent's disease,* after French physician Jean-Hyacinthe Vincent, who first described it. The formal name for it is *acute necrotizing ulcerative gingivitis*, or *ANUG*.

Cause: The disease apparently does not result from an invasion of some foreign germ but from the sudden, explosive growth of the normal bacteria in the mouth. It is triggered by physical fatigue, psychological stress, poor diet, poor dental hygiene, and smoking.

Incidence: Trench mouth tends to occur most often among young adults and those with weakened immune systems, such as AIDS patients and cancer patients undergoing chemotherapy.

Noticeable symptoms: The inflammation of the gums is usually severe and painful. It may cause a foul taste and bad breath and be accompanied by a fever.

Diagnosis: Cultures of scrapings from the gums are likely to reveal the bacteria that typically provoke the inflammation.

Treatment options: Conservative treatment includes careful cleaning of the teeth and gums, rinsing with salt water or gentle antiseptics, painkillers, and rest. Antibiotics are sometimes used to reduce the population of bacteria.

Gargle saltwater

Outlook: When trench mouth is promptly treated, the inflammation subsides, and recovery is usually complete. Untreated, the condition may result in permanent damage to the gums and other tissues of the mouth and face.

Prevention: Regular brushing and flossing and the use of antiseptic rinses can help keep the population under control.

Trichinosis
(TRIHK-uh-NOH-sihs)

DISEASE

TYPE: PARASITIC

Eating undercooked or inadequately smoked meat, especially pork, increases the risk of being infected with trichina worms and developing trichinosis. These tiny worms can cause serious illness. Fortunately, however, this illness can easily be prevented.

Cause: Trichinosis is caused by *Trichinella spiralis*, a small parasite belonging to a group of worms called nematodes, or roundworms. The worm larvas live in protective cysts in the muscles of certain animals, such as pigs. When a person eats

See also
Food poisoning
Parasites and disease

undercooked and infested meat, the larvas enter the person's intestines. There the larvas are freed from the cysts and mature into adult worms. The adults reproduce: Each female may produce 1,000 or more larvas. These larvas pass from the intestines into the blood. Those that enter skeletal muscles—particularly muscles in the tongue, diaphragm, chest, and eye area—form cysts. The cysts can survive for up to 30 years.

Noticeable symptoms: Within a day or two of eating infested meat a person may experience vomiting and diarrhea. After another one to two weeks, as new larvas move through the body, the upper eyelids become swollen. This may be followed by muscle pains, fever, chills, thirst, fatigue, and weakness. ***See a physician if these symptoms develop, especially after eating undercooked meat.***

Diagnosis: A doctor will confirm a diagnosis of trichinosis by taking a blood sample and performing a count of white blood cells called eosinophils (EE-uh-SIHN-uh-fihlz), which increase in response to the infestation.

Treatment options: Antiparasitic medicines such as thiabendazole may be prescribed to kill adult worms and larvas in the intestines. Corticosteroids and painkillers may be prescribed to combat various symptoms. Bed rest will be strongly recommended.

Stages and progress: After the larvas become encysted, symptoms gradually disappear.

Prevention: To avoid getting trichinosis, pork, pork products, and meat from wild game should be thoroughly cooked. This will kill any larvas that may be present.

Phone doctor

Rest

Trichomonas

(TRIHK-uh-MON-uhs)

DISEASE

TYPE: INFECTIOUS (PARASITIC)

The disease most people call trichomonas is also known as *trich*. The formal name of this STD (sexually transmitted disease) is *trichomoniasis* (TRIHK-uh-muh-NIY-uh-sihs), which means infestation by the trichomonas parasite.

Cause: *Trichomonas vaginalis* is a single-celled protozoan that thrives in the moist environment of the human reproductive

Avoid alcohol

tract. The infection occurs primarily in the urethra of men and the vagina of women.

Incidence: Trichomoniasis affects an estimated 2 to 3 million people in the United States each year. Most diagnosed cases are in 16- to 35-year-old women.

Noticeable symptoms: As with other STDs, the symptoms differ in women and men.

About 60% of infected women have a thick yellow-green to gray discharge from the vagina, vaginal odor, painful urination, and painful intercourse. They may also suffer from lower abdominal pain.

Men may have a water-clear discharge from the penis and painful urination, but it is more common for men to have no symptoms at all.

Diagnosis: Examining samples of the fluid from the vagina or penis under a microscope may show the protozoans, but a more reliable method, especially for infected men, is to place a sample of the fluid on culture medium to grow the protozoans.

Treatment options: Antiprotozoal medication—that is, a drug designed to kill protozoans—is prescribed to kill the parasite. Both partners should be treated at the same time so that one does not remain infected and reinfect the treated partner. Antiprotozoal medication, however, blocks the breakdown of alcohol, causing nausea and abdominal pain if the patient drinks during treatment.

Stages and progress: Symptoms usually appear four to 20 days after infestation, but may not occur until years later in some individuals. Most women who show symptoms usually do so within 6 months of infection.

There are few known complications of trichomonas, but it may increase the likelihood of HIV infection, and, in pregnant women it may result in premature delivery and low birth-weight babies.

Prevention: Trichomonas can be transmitted if a person is infected even if there are no symptoms. The best prevention, after abstinence, is the use of latex condoms. This is not 100% effective but is much safer than having sex without a barrier.

Trigeminal neuralgia

(triy-JEHM-uh-nuhl noo-RAAL-juh)

DISEASE

TYPE: MECHANICAL (?)

See also
Hypertension
Multiple sclerosis
Neuralgia
Pain
Tic

The two trigeminal ("three-branched") nerves are the main sensory nerves of the face. Each is connected to one side of the brain stem. Irritation of a trigeminal nerve may trigger trigeminal neuralgia, an attack of severe pain on the side of the face served by the nerve. Sometimes the pain sets off involuntary spasms in nearby muscles, causing a facial twitch, or tic. The intense pain is often called *tic douloureux*.

Cause: The basic cause is unknown. In some cases the nerve is disturbed by the pressure of a nearby blood vessel against the nerve root. About 1 to 2% of persons with multiple sclerosis develop trigeminal neuralgia as one symptom. Hypertension is apparently a risk factor also.

Incidence: In the United States perhaps 40,000 persons experience trigeminal neuralgia. It is concentrated among people over the age of 50, and 50% more women than men are affected.

Noticeable symptoms: An attack occurs suddenly, producing severe, stabbing pain, usually on one side of the face. It lasts from a few seconds to a minute or so and is followed by a lingering sting and tenderness that may last several minutes. The pain may occur anywhere from the forehead to the chin, but most often around the nose, cheeks, and mouth. Attacks are likely to be triggered by harmless stimuli, such as light touch, changes in temperature, and the sensations that accompany talking or chewing. Some people take elaborate measures to avoid disturbing these trigger points; for example, they may stop washing or brushing their hair, brushing their teeth, or shaving.

Diagnosis: There is no special test for trigeminal neuralgia. Diagnosis is based on the patient's description of the distinctive symptoms.

Treatment options: The disease can usually be controlled by drugs. The most widely used are the anticonvulsant drugs used to treat epilepsy. Antidepressants and a muscle relaxant called baclofen can also be helpful.

In certain severe cases surgery is used to remove the pressure of a blood vessel on the nerve root. A small pad of inert material is inserted to separate the blood vessel from the nerve.

Tropical diseases

The warm, moist climate of the tropics provides an ideal medium for many living things, from tiny microorganisms to very large plants and animals. Not only are there more of these living things in a tropical rain forest, but the favorable conditions also foster a wider diversity of organisms—including disease-causing species.

Spreading the diseases: A tropical rain forest teems with insects and other arthropods. Insects that bite people—mosquitoes, flies, fleas, lice, and ticks—provide effective ways for diseases to move from one human to another or between animals and humans. The English scientist Patrick Manson was the first to discover this in the late 1870s, when he proved mosquitoes spread elephantiasis to humans. He also theorized that mosquitoes transmit malaria to humans, which was later proved to be the case. Since then many tropical diseases have been linked to insect carriers. Mosquitoes, for example, also transmit dengue fever, yellow fever, Rift Valley fever, and West Nile virus. Biting flies can carry African sleeping sickness, various forms of leishmaniasis (LEESH-muh-NIY-uh-sihs, sandfly fever), and river blindness. Mites, fleas, lice, and ticks transmit plague and typhus, among other diseases.

In South America one of the more serious tropical diseases is *Chagas* (SHAH-guhs) *disease*—also called *American trypanosomiasis* (trih-PAAN-uh-soh-MIY-uh-sihs). It kills thousands of persons each year and infects millions. As the name *trypanosomiasis* suggests, it is caused by a trypanosome. It has similar symptoms to African sleeping sickness, also caused by trypanosomes. In this case the insect that spreads the parasite is the "kissing bug" *Triatoma infestans*, which often bites humans at night.

New mosquito-borne diseases become apparent to Western observers on a regular basis. Many of these are caused by viruses called *arboviruses*, a group of viruses that are endemic in insects and other arthropods, such as ticks. The infections tend to be similar to encephalitis, dengue, or hemorrhagic fevers. In Brazil's tropical rain forest some 183 new arboviruses have been located, including one that causes Rocio encephalitis and one that causes Sibiá hemorrhagic fever. The disease o'*nygong-nyong* appeared in Uganda in 1959 and affected millions of people in Central and East Africa. Another East African virus of this type causes *chikungunya*. These diseases are each carried by different species of tropical mosquitoes—o'nygong-nyong on the *Anopheles* mosquitoes well known for malaria, and chikungunya on the *Aedes aegypti* mosquitoes known for dengue and yellow fever. The Congo arbovirus is spread by ticks and causes a hemorrhagic fever. Unlike most tropical diseases, Congo virus also has produced an outbreak in the temperate Crimean peninsula.

Our primate cousins: There is a rich body of evidence that humans originated in Africa and that they have inhabited that continent and nearby Asia much longer than anywhere else on Earth. Both continents have large tropical regions, providing millions of years for humans and tropical diseases to evolve together. Furthermore, our closest relatives, the primates (apes, monkeys, lemurs, and so forth) live mostly in the tropics.

Many diseases do not depend on human hosts alone for their survival. Although yellow fever, for example, has been largely eradicated, eliminating the disease altogether is probably impossible in the tropics. Our primate cousins, monkeys and marmosets, in Brazil and Africa also host yellow fever. They are reservoirs of the disease. Mosquitoes that live in Brazil and Africa transmit the yellow fever virus from animal to animal and occasionally to people living and working there.

Ebola is a mysterious and frightening disease that medical scientists have just begun to grapple with. No one knows what animal is its natural reservoir, but people have developed the disease from contact with chimpanzees. Ebola is similar to another hemorrhagic fever, *Marburg disease,* named after an outbreak in 1967 in Marburg, Germany, that was traced to a shipment of African green monkeys from Uganda. Ebola first appeared in 1976 in Zaire and the Sudan. Even HIV, the virus that causes AIDS, has its closest relatives in a disease that affects chimpanzees.

World travel: At one time tropical diseases were primarily the concern of those who live in the tropics. Today jet aircraft whisk large numbers of people from continent to continent, often bringing diseases with them.

Tuberculosis

(too-BUR-kyuh-LO-sihs)

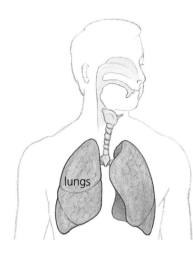

lungs

Dangers from TB

In most cases the tuberculosis bacteria settle in the lungs, causing a characteristic cough, fever, and paleness. Less often the bacteria affect the bones or brain, where they produce widespread damage.

Tuberculosis (TB) killed more people in the United States during the nineteenth century than any other disease. Improvements in housing and nutrition in the early twentieth century slowed the spread of TB. Effective medicines developed in the 1940s and 1950s decreased the deadliness of the disease; more than 90% of patients survive with appropriate medical care. Despite this, tuberculosis remains a leading cause of death in the world because of its prevalence in developing regions.

Cause: TB is caused by bacteria—*Mycobacterium tuberculosis*. They can live in any organ of the body, but usually the lungs are affected. When a person is sick with TB of the lungs, bacteria are expelled into the air in tiny particles of sputum whenever the person coughs or sneezes. These tiny particles can hang in the air for long periods of time and be inhaled by others. Despite the fact that TB is transmitted through the air, it is difficult to become infected.

Incidence: In the United States cases of TB declined until the mid-1980s, then began to rise. In 1992 there were 26,673 cases of TB; but by 2000 this had decreased to 16,000, of whom about a thousand died from the disease.

The number of reported cases of TB is the number of people who become sick; they are said to have *active TB* and can infect others if the active infection is in the lungs. Many other people—an estimated 15 million in the United States—have TB bacteria in their bodies but are not ill and cannot pass the bacteria to anyone else. A person infected with TB but healthy, however, has a 5 to 10% chance of developing active TB.

Noticeable symptoms: The first symptoms of TB include fever, night sweats, lack of appetite, and weight loss. As the disease progresses chest pain and a cough occur, then bloody sputum accompanies the cough.

Diagnosis: A chest x-ray reveals damage to the lungs caused when the bacteria multiply and spread. A sputum sample can be cultured to see if *Mycobacterium* bacteria are present. The bacteria grow very slowly, and it takes four weeks for the culture to confirm TB bacteria. A *skin test* will indicate in two days whether or not a person's body has TB bacteria.

Treatment options: TB is treated with a combination of antibiotics. After a few weeks of treatment, if tests show that the person is no longer infectious, the patient can return to normal life. However, the treatment must continue for six to twelve months to be sure that all of the bacteria are destroyed.

When a case of active TB is diagnosed, all the people who have had contact with the ill person should be given the skin test. Those who are positive, even if not ill, may also be treated with antibiotics.

Stages and progress: TB bacteria ride tiny particles into the lungs of the person inhaling them. Many bacteria are killed immediately by the immune system, but some survive and multiply. After several weeks to several months the immune system confines all remaining bacteria to little gray granules called *tubercles* (TOO-buhr-kuhlz) in the lungs. The patient will have a positive TB skin test but not be made ill by the bacteria.

If the immune system begins to work less well, because of aging, poor nutrition or living conditions, cancer, infections such as HIV, or other causes, the bacteria can break out of the tubercles and spread to other areas of the lungs. The immune system fights back, killing bacteria and surrounding cells. The earliest symptoms start at about this stage. Over time more and more of the lungs are damaged. Cavities can form and break through into the bronchi, releasing bacteria that can be coughed out. If untreated, the destruction of the lungs continues, resulting in death in 40 to 60% of cases.

Effects on world population and health: Globally, TB kills 1.6 million people each year. The World Health Organization estimates that 1 billion new infections will occur between 2000 and 2020 if TB controls are not improved. The global TB epidemic is accelerating because of HIV infection and inadequate treatment of active TB in many parts of the world.

A vaccine, BCG, is used in many parts of the world, but not in the United States. When given to babies, BCG prevents the spread of TB bacteria in the body but does not prevent infection. In adults BCG provides only limited protection. Researchers in many areas of the world are trying to create both a better vaccine and more effective medications to reduce the human devastation of TB.

Tularemia

(too-luh-REE-mee-uh)

DISEASE

TYPE: INFECTIOUS
(BACTERIAL)

See also
Animal diseases and humans
Bacteria and disease

Phone doctor

Tularemia is sometimes called *rabbit fever* or *deerfly fever*—names that give clues to how it is spread from animals to humans. It is highly contagious, but simple preventive measures can help to avoid the disease.

Cause: Tularemia is caused by the bacterium *Francisella tularensis*. People can become infected by handling infected wild rodents and rabbits. People also can become infected through bites from infected blood-sucking arthropods, especially ticks and deerflies.

Incidence: Tularemia is named for Tulare County in California, where it was first identified in ground squirrels in 1911. It occurs throughout the northern hemisphere. Farmers, hunters, trappers, butchers, and game wardens are among those at greatest risk of contracting the disease.

Noticeable symptoms: Symptoms usually appear within five days following exposure. If tularemia is caused by a bite or from bacteria entering a cut, the most common symptom is a red spot at the point of entry. Ingesting food or water containing the bacteria may produce coughing, stomach pain, diarrhea, and vomiting. Other symptoms include swollen lymph glands, fever, chills, and headaches. ***It is important to see a doctor; without treatment tularemia can be fatal.***

Diagnosis: A physician will suspect tularemia if a person has had contact with rodents or rabbits or been bitten by a tick or insect. Samples of tissue from the lesion or from lymph nodes may be taken and examined for *Francisella tularensis*. Blood tests can indicate the presence of antibodies produced in response to the bacteria.

Treatment options: Tularemia can be effectively treated with antibiotics such as streptomycin and gentamicin. Once recovered, there is a lifelong immunity to the disease.

Prevention: Tularemia is very contagious. People who handle wild rodents and rabbits should wear protective clothing. Ticks should be removed immediately; the skin should be checked for tick bites and the characteristic red spot. Wild animals should be thoroughly cooked before eating.

Tumor, benign

Unlike cancerous (malignant) tumors, benign growths remain in a compact mass and do not spread to other parts of the body. Their cells appear under the microscope like those of normal tissue—which cancer cells do not. Benign tumors occur anywhere in the body and sometimes become quite large.

Cause: Division of cells in normal tissue is usually restrained after the body has completed its period of normal growth. Cells commonly then divide only often enough to replace those that die. In a benign tumor the restraining mechanism fails, and the affected cells continue dividing. Eventually, the mass of cells becomes big enough to be recognized as a distinct tumor.

Incidence: Benign tumors are fairly common. Among the many places where they occur are in the breasts, bones, muscles, spinal cord, intestines, uterus, larynx, and bladder.

Noticeable symptoms: Symptoms vary with the location of the tumor. They may be no more than a noticeable lump. Other symptoms reflect disturbance of body processes (see list below).

Diagnosis: A doctor will take a sample of the tumor tissue (a biopsy) for tests to determine if the tumor is benign or cancerous.

Treatment options: If the tumor is large enough to interfere with the normal functioning of nearby organs, it will be removed surgically. No further treatment will be needed.

Some types of benign tumor: Several tumor types are especially well known. These are removed surgically if possible.

- *Acoustic neuroma:* A tumor of the nerve that leads to the inner ear. It affects balance and hearing.
- *Adenoma* (AAD-n-OH-muh): A tumor on a gland. This often causes disease by production of too much or too little of the product of that gland. Fibroadenomas are benign lumps in breast tissue.
- *Central nervous system tumor:* A tumor of the brain or spinal cord. Although 70% of such tumors are benign, they affect mental or body processes because of pressure on nerves, since both brain and spinal column are tightly enclosed in bone.

- *Fibroid* (FIY-broid) *tumor:* A benign tumor of the uterus made primarily of fibrous tissue. If small enough, it is left in place. Large fibroids can interfere with pregnancy or press on nearby organs and are usually removed.
- *Lipoma* (lih-POH-muh)*:* A fatty tumor or a soft lump growing on the skin or elsewhere. It usually causes no physical difficulty.

Typhoid fever
(TIY-foid)

DISEASE

TYPE: INFECTIOUS
(BACTERIAL)

See also
Constipation
Diarrhea
Fever
Food poisoning
Paratyphoid fever
Pneumonia
Salmonella

Phone doctor

Typhoid, or typhoid fever or *enteric* (ehn-TEHR-ihk) *fever,* is a serious disease that is now relatively rare in the United States and other developed countries. Essentially a virulent form of food poisoning, it causes a debilitating fever and other symptoms.

Cause: The bacterium *Salmonella typhi* causes typhoid. When contaminated food or liquids are ingested, the bacteria enter the lymph system through the intestines. Multiplying typhoid bacteria then cause the fever and other symptoms.

Incidence: Typhoid is rare in the United States, and only about 600 cases a year are reported. Outbreaks occur in developing countries. Typhoid is famous for carriers, such as Typhoid Mary, who was linked to more than 50 cases of the disease from 1906 to 1932, although Typhoid Mary herself was never ill.

Noticeable symptoms: A week or more after exposure, flulike symptoms and a fever spiking as high as 105°F begin. ***Always see a physician for high fevers.*** Most patients become constipated, then experience diarrhea. Pink blotches appear on the skin several days after other symptoms. Complications occur often in untreated typhoid, including pneumonia, bleeding in the stomach or intestine, and infection of vital organs.

Diagnosis: Blood, urine, and stool samples can reveal the bacterium.

Treatment options: Antibiotics are effective against the typhoid bacteria and, given early enough, can prevent the disease from entering advanced stages. Intravenous feeding may be necessary if the disease has progressed to the point at which stomach bleeding and burst intestines might be caused by food ingestion. Even so, 98% of those infected eventually recover.

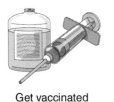

Get vaccinated

Wash hands

Prevention: A vaccine that can help immunize a person against typhoid is available for travelers in areas where the disease is prevalent. Proper sanitation measures for handling food, for water supplies, and for waste disposal are the best overall methods of preventing the spread of typhoid, however.

Typhus

(TIY-fuhs)

DISEASE

TYPE: INFECTIOUS
(BACTERIAL)

See also
Animal diseases and humans
Bacteria and disease
Rashes
Rocky Mountain spotted fever

Any of several potentially serious fevers caused by rickettsia bacteria that are spread by body lice, fleas, and mites are called typhus (also *prison fever* or *ship fever*). Epidemic typhus, spread by lice, is the most common form; it has caused severe epidemics in the past.

Cause: A very small bacterium called *Rickettsia prowazekii* causes epidemic typhus. The lice get the disease by biting an infected human; eventually they are killed by the organism as it multiplies. But where people are crowded together and where hygiene is poor, the infected lice can spread to other human hosts before they die.

Incidence: Typhus is rare in the United States—incidence in most years is fewer than 20 cases. Elsewhere epidemic typhus can be found where people are living in overcrowded conditions, especially where sanitation is poor and vermin that spread the disease can flourish. It continues to be common on battlefields during local wars.

Murine typhus or *endemic typhus* is a less common and milder form of the disease. It is spread by rat or mouse fleas. Most cases in the United States occur in southern Texas and California.

Scrub typhus is transmitted to humans by mites found on field mice. Without medical treatment scrub typhus can produce serious complications and death rates upward of 30%. Timely administration of antibiotics all but eliminates fatalities, however. Scrub typhus is common in eastern Asia.

Noticeable symptoms: The first symptoms of epidemic typhus include cough, chest pain, severe headache, and nausea. A high fever, chills, muscle aches, a rash in all but about 10% of the cases, diarrhea or constipation, and vomiting follow soon after.

Diagnosis: A diagnosis of typhus can be confirmed by a blood test. The presence of specific antibodies in the blood will identify the particular type.

Treatment options: Antibiotics have proven effective for treating all types of typhus. One of the important early steps in treatment is to rid the patient's body of the lice or mites that caused the disease in the first place. Once that is done and the patient's clothes have been treated and washed, the infection cannot spread from the patient. People who were living in close proximity to the patient will have to undergo similar sanitary measures, however, if the spread of typhus is to be stopped.

Stages and progress: It may take anywhere from a week to two weeks after exposure for the first symptoms of epidemic typhus to develop. The fever, rash, and other symptoms appear a few days later. As the fever worsens, the patient may become confused and delirious. Without treatment the fever may cause the patient to slip into a coma and die. The red rash that comes with the fever starts on the patient's torso and then spreads outward to all parts of the body but the face, palms, and soles of the feet. There may be bleeding from the rash.

Typhus is usually not fatal, especially when medical treatment is available. Deaths associated with the disease often involve complications, such as pneumonia, or prior medical conditions that have weakened the patient. The elderly are most often at risk.

Prevention: No commercial vaccine is available. Individuals who travel to places where typhus is common should take personal preventive measures. These include bathing frequently, changing underclothes often, and disinfecting and washing clothing to kill lice and their eggs.

U

Ulcerative colitis   *See* **Colitis; Irritable bowel syndrome**

Ulcers

(UL-suhrs)

DISEASE

TYPE: INFECTIOUS (BACTERIAL)

Phone doctor

See also
Bacteria and disease
Cancers
Esophagus
Peritonitis
Small intestine
Tumor, benign

Emergency Room

Ulcers are any open sores in the skin or the lining of an organ, but in most cases the ulcers referred to are *peptic ulcers,* or sores in the lining of the upper digestive tract. Ulcers are fairly common and usually not life-threatening, but serious complications can result. ***Get prompt medical treatment if you suspect you have an ulcer;*** early detection and treatment may mean a quicker recovery and less risk of complications.

The three most common places people get ulcers are the esophagus, the stomach, and the duodenum, which is the short section of small intestine directly connected to the stomach. Stomach ulcers are often called *gastric* (GAAS-trihk) *ulcers.*

Complete perforation of the stomach or intestinal wall is one of the potentially serious complications of an ulcer. Peritonitis, a serious internal infection, may develop with a perforated ulcer, making this situation a medical emergency. Another complication can be bleeding from the ulcer. If the bleeding is severe, the patient may go into shock; slow bleeding over a long period of time may result in anemia. Another complication that may arise from certain types of chronic ulcers is scar tissue that builds until it obstructs the opening from the stomach to the intestine.

Cause: Physicians once thought excess stomach acid caused almost all peptic ulcers, but recent studies have shown that a bacterium called *Helicobacter pylori* causes most stomach and duodenal ulcers. The bacteria are often present in a person's digestive tract, but in about one person in six where they are present the bacteria cause the breakdown in the protective mucous lining that results in an ulcer.

Another major cause of ulcers is the use of aspirin, ibuprofen, and other nonsteroidal anti-inflammatory drugs (NSAIDs). For some reason these drugs cause breaks in the protective mucous lining.

Certain types of tumors in the duodenum or pancreas may also cause ulcers by stimulating the production of excess acids. This condition is called *Zollinger-Ellison syndrome.*

Incidence: About one in every ten Americans will develop a peptic ulcer. About 4 million Americans have gastric ulcers. African Americans and Hispanic Americans are twice as likely to have ulcers as

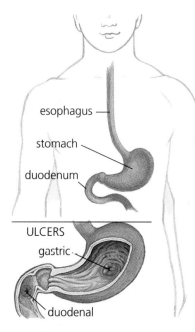

Sites for ulcers
Digestive system ulcers primarily attack the stomach and duodenum, where acids and digestive juices are most powerful, but they can also affect the lower esophagus.

Avoid aspirin

other Americans. The most common ulcers are in the duodenum—*duodenal* (DOO-uh-DEE-nuhl) *ulcers*—and they appear most often when the patient is between 40 and 50 years of age. Stomach ulcers appear most frequently between the ages of 60 and 70.

Noticeable symptoms: A periodic gnawing, burning, or hungry feeling in the upper abdomen or under the breastbone is a common symptom. Pain halfway up the back is also possible if there is an ulcer on the back of the duodenum; however, in some cases there is no pain or discomfort at all. For a duodenal ulcer, eating usually eases the discomfort. For a gastric ulcer, eating either worsens the pain or has no effect on it. The pain often troubles the patient for a few days or weeks and then disappears for periods lasting weeks or months. Bloating and nausea after meals is another possible symptom. With a bleeding ulcer the feces may turn black and tarry and have an unusual foul smell. Maroon-colored stools and vomiting up red or coffee-ground-colored material are also signs of bleeding.

Diagnosis: Tests will be needed to confirm the diagnosis of an ulcer and to determine where it is located. A simple blood test can determine if *Helicobacter pylori* bacteria is present in the body. Although a barium x-ray has long been used to detect peptic ulcers, it is more common today to examine the stomach with upper endoscopy—using a small, lighted tube passed through the mouth to view (and perhaps sample tissue from) the esophagus, stomach, and duodenum. Sample tissue from the stomach will be checked by a pathologist to make sure that sores seen with endoscopy are not caused by stomach cancer.

Treatment options: For most ulcers treatment involves a course of antibiotics to eliminate the *Helicobacter pylori* bacteria and medications to counteract stomach acids and to decrease acid production until the ulcer has healed. Where long-term aspirin use (or other similar medications associated with ulcer formation) is involved, switching to a nonirritating medication usually brings about a quick recovery. When patients cannot switch for medical reasons, there is a drug (misoprostol) that effectively prevents formation of this type of ulcer.

Prevention: Avoiding regular use of aspirin and other NSAIDs can help prevent ulcers in some people.

Uterus

(YOO-tuhr-uhs)

BODY SYSTEM

See also
Birth canal
Cancers
Cervical and uterine cancers
Menstrual pain
PID (pelvic inflammatory disease)
Reproductive system
Tumor, benign

The uterus is often known by its old English name of *womb*. It is where an embryo settles after fertilization of an egg and where it grows into a baby.

Size and location: The uterus is a pear-shaped and pear-sized organ located in the middle of a woman's body at the top of the birth canal, just above the bladder. During pregnancy the uterus expands considerably. The location above the bladder causes women who are pregnant to need to urinate more frequently.

Role: When an egg, or *ovum*, is fertilized, it attaches itself to the lining of the uterus, which is a special tissue called the *endometrium*. If a normal pregnancy develops, both the fetus and placenta remain within a much expanded uterus until birth.

Conditions that affect the uterus: The most dramatic condition that affects the uterus is *pregnancy*. During a woman's reproductive years most women, in months that they are not pregnant, shed the lining of the uterus, which is called *menstruation*.

The uterus is subject to several kinds of tumor. *Fibroids* (FIY-broidz) are benign tumors that seldom threaten life. But larger fibroids or painful ones may need to be removed by a surgical procedure called *dilatation and curettage* (DIHL-uh-TAY-shuhn, KYOOR-ih-TAHZH) *(D & C)* in which the lining of the uterus is scraped or, if no further pregnancies are desired, by removal of the uterus. Uterine cancer is second only to cancer of the cervix in frequency for cancer of the reproductive system in women. It is more common in older women who have not had children. Because it grows slowly, it is less dangerous than many other cancers. Bleeding after menopause is a common early warning sign.

A common disorder that often requires no treatment is inflammation or irritation of the lining of the uterus. This condition, called *endometritis* (EHN-doh-meh-TRIY-tihs), may be treated with D & C if it is causing pain or other problems. Infection of the uterus, which often spreads to other reproductive organs, is called PID (pelvic inflammatory disease).

The muscles that hold the uterus and vagina in place sometimes become weakened by childbirth or by age. If the uterus begins to sag, it may bulge into the wall of the vagina, a condition called *prolapse* (sometimes known as "fallen womb").

Several congenital disorders can affect the position or shape of the uterus. Unless the uterus is not present—which can occur—these make conception more difficult but not impossible.

Uveitis

(YOO-vee-IY-tihs)

DISEASE

TYPE: INFLAMMATORY;
      AUTOIMMUNE

See also

AIDS (acquired immunodeficiency syndrome)
Autoimmune diseases
Cataract
Colitis
Crohn's disease
Glaucoma
Kawasaki disease
Psoriasis
Rheumatoid arthritis
Sarcoidosis
Shingles
Syphilis
Tuberculosis

Phone doctor

Uveitis is a potentially serious inflammation of the *uvea* (YOO-vee-uh), a layer of tissue in the eye. The uvea lies just under the eye's outer layer, or *sclera* (SKLEHR-uh), and includes the *iris,* the colored portion of the eye, along with muscles for sizing the pupil and blood vessels that supply the retina. Inflammation may be limited to just the front or only the back part of the eye. Sometimes the disease inflames the complete uvea in one or both eyes.

Cause: Among the diseases that can infect the uvea are herpes, chicken pox or shingles, tuberculosis, Lyme disease, syphilis, and toxoplasmosis. Often uveitis of the front of the eye results from the immune system attacking tissue there—an autoimmune reaction. Rheumatoid arthritis, sarcoidosis, and Crohn's disease are also autoimmune diseases and often occur at the same time as uveitis.

Physical injury to the uvea and allergic reactions may also lead to uveitis.

Noticeable symptoms: Blurred vision, pain, sensitivity to light, and redness of the affected eye are common symptoms when the uvea at the front of the eye is inflamed. When only the back of the eye is affected, symptoms may be limited to blurred vision and floaters, small specs in the field of vision.

Diagnosis: The pupil (the opening in the iris) will be small and sometimes irregularly shaped. Inflammation of parts of the retina may be present.

Treatment options: Swelling of the uvea can be reduced with steroid ointments, drops, or injections. A drug to keep the pupil dilated may also be prescribed. Immunosuppressant drugs are sometimes used as well.

Stages and progress: Prompt medical treatment of uveitis is very important because serious complications, including glaucoma, cataracts, or loss of vision, may develop.

Vaccination and disease

Two hundred years ago the English physician Edward Jenner noticed that milkmaids frequently got a mild disease called cowpox from the cows in their care. But during smallpox epidemics these young women were protected and did not become ill. Jenner used these observations to develop the first vaccine against a contagious disease.

Today vaccination against disease remains one of the most effective ways to improve public and personal health by protecting against some diseases caused by bacteria and viruses. Efforts to develop vaccines against parasites have so far failed, but work continues with some hope for success.

How vaccination works: People can sometimes become immune to a disease by becoming ill with the disease and surviving it. If the microorganisms causing that disease invade the body again, the immune system remembers and quickly destroys them without the person becoming ill for a second time.

A vaccination accomplishes the same thing but without the initial illness. The vaccination stimulates immunity to a disease by exposing the immune system to live, but weakened, organisms or to dead or inactivated organisms. In some newer vaccines genetically engineered parts of the germ are used to stimulate the immune system. The immune system responds and creates a molecular "memory" of the disease organism. This memory is kept by special white blood cells. If a subsequent invasion by the same germ occurs, the immune system causes those white blood cells to multiply quickly and to defend against the disease. As a result the vaccinated person either remains healthy or has only mild symptoms.

Vaccination has some risks. Occasionally, individuals develop symptoms related to the vaccination. Most common are allergic reactions to the medium in which the microorganisms are grown. People with problems of the immune system, such as AIDS, may not be able to have vaccinations made with live organisms.

Effective vaccinations have been developed to protect

Get vaccinated

against many diseases, including smallpox, measles, mumps, chicken pox, tetanus, rubella, polio, and diphtheria. Some vaccinations are given in a single dose, either orally or by injection, while others require multiple doses over a prescribed time period to provide maximum benefit. Most types of vaccination require a booster shot periodically as a kind of reminder to the immune system. Influenza vaccinations are given annually because each year different strains of influenza occur. Vaccination to protect against pneumococcal pneumonia is recommended for everyone over 65 years of age.

Vaccination requirements: In the United States vaccination against childhood disease is required for entry into grade school. This public health requirement has dramatically reduced cases of measles, mumps, rubella, polio, diphtheria, tetanus, and pertussis (whooping cough). In the mid-1990s two new vaccinations were added: hepatitis B and *Hemophilus influenzae* type B (Hib). In 2001 it was recommended that young children be vaccinated for chicken pox, hepatitis A, pneumonia, and influenza. It was also recommended that children already in school be vaccinated against hepatitis B.

In underdeveloped and developing countries vaccinations have not been as available as in developed countries. In 1995, 11 million children under the age of five died in undeveloped nations. Nine million of these deaths were due to infectious diseases, and 25% of these could have been prevented if the children had been vaccinated.

Future directions: Vaccination is the single most powerful method to control contagious diseases. Researchers are searching for new or improved vaccines for tuberculosis, syphilis, HIV (AIDS), encephalitis, meningitis, anthrax, and other diseases. New techniques, including genetic engineering, are being explored to develop better, safer, and less expensive vaccines.

Vaccination offers real hope for eliminating specific contagious diseases from the planet. Smallpox, the deadly epidemic disease that killed millions and inspired Jenner, was declared eradicated in 1980. Global vaccination efforts may be able to repeat this achievement. The World Health Organization reported in 2001 that all but ten countries are now free of polio. They are working to have polio eradicated by 2005.

Vaginitis

(VAAJ-uh-NIY-tihs)

DISEASE

TYPE: BACTERIAL;
PARASITICAL; FUNGAL

See also
Bacteria and disease
Candidiasis
Immune system
PID (pelvic inflammatory disease)
STD (sexually transmitted diseases)
Trichomonas

Any vaginal infection that causes inflammation is known as vaginitis; it may lead to the more serious PID (pelvic inflammatory disease) if untreated.

Cause: Many different microorganisms can cause an infection of the vagina, including the protist parasite trichomonas and the fungal yeast *Candida* (KAAN-dih-duh). The most common cause of vaginitis, however, is runaway multiplication of one or another species of bacteria (or perhaps several at once), a condition termed *bacterial vaginosis* (VAAJ-uh-NOH-sihs) or BV. BV appears to result when the ecological balance maintained by the usual bacteria in the vagina changes; that is, some aggressive bacterium species grows rapidly at the expense of the others. Vaginal inflammation may also result from allergies.

Incidence: An estimated one woman in three will have some form of vaginitis in her lifetime. Although vaginitis can be sexually transmitted, often it is not.

Noticeable symptoms: Intense itching and swelling of the vulva or vagina or both are often the first symptoms of infection. BV has a variety of other symptoms, depending on the cause; common ones are an abnormal discharge from the vagina that may have a fishy odor, discomfort or burning during urination, and discomfort during sexual intercourse. About half of women with vaginitis have no symptoms.

Diagnosis: A physician may observe the symptoms during an examination or, in the case of BV, may find cells from the vaginal lining coated with bacteria ("clue cells") during a microscopic examination of vaginal fluid.

Treatment options: Antibiotic therapy is used to treat BV, antiprotozoal medication—designed to kill protozoans—is used for trichomonas, and antifungal medication is used for candidiasis. Sometimes lowering the bacterial population with antibiotics will allow *Candida* to multiply and bring vaginitis back from a different cause; eating yogurt with live bacteria during antibiotic therapy is a home remedy to counter this side effect of antibiotics. The *Lactobacillus* bacterium that is a normal inhabitant of the vagina is in the same family as that used to ferment yogurt.

Valley fever

DISEASE

TYPE: INFECTIOUS (FUNGAL)

Phone doctor

There are several diseases caused by a fungus invading a human body. In the United States the most common of such diseases is usually known as valley fever because it was encountered by early settlers in the San Joaquin Valley of California. Its official name is *coccidioidomycosis* (kok-SIHD-ee-oi-doh-miy-KOH-sihs); it is also called *desert fever, desert rheumatism,* and *San Joaquin Valley fever.* Although coccidioidomycosis has been known for a long time, its increase in recent years classifies it as an emerging disease.

Cause: The fungus *Coccidoides immitis* lives in sand or soil; its spores can be blown about by the wind and then inhaled by humans. The fungus grows in the lungs and releases forms that thrive in humans—if they can get past immune mechanisms that thwart them 60% of the time.

Incidence: Valley fever normally affects 50,000 to 100,000 people in the United States each year, mostly in dry regions of the Southwest. In regions where the disease is endemic, about 3% of the population develop the disease annually. About 50 to 100 people die of the disease each year in the United States. African Americans, Filipinos, pregnant women, and people with compromised immunity are at special risk.

Coccidioidomycosis is also found in dry, hot regions of Central and South America.

Noticeable symptoms: If the fungus succeeds in establishing itself in the lungs, it causes fatigue, chest pain, fever, headache, a rash on the legs, night sweats, muscle aches, and cough. This may go away after a few weeks and then reappear. Some people, especially children, develop a red, blotchy rash on the palms, soles of the feet, and folds in the groin. For a person who lives in or has recently visited the Southwest or dry regions on the West Coast, Central America, or South America, valley fever may be suspected if the symptoms persist for more than two weeks. ***See a physician for a definite diagnosis.*** Pregnant women or people with ineffective immune systems should report flulike symptoms as soon as they occur.

If later complications develop, symptoms may include low appetite and weight loss; blood in saliva; skin sores; and pain in the bones and joints, similar to that of arthritis. The most serious complication is meningitis.

Diagnosis: A skin test can indicate exposure to the fungus, but it is not sufficient to diagnose the disease. A physician will want to test body fluids, such as sputum, for definite signs. A diagnosis can be confirmed only by finding spores in body fluid, although the fungus can also be observed on chest x-rays.

Treatment options: In most cases the disease is self-limiting; the immune system wins, and the fungus is eliminated from the body without any outside intervention. If the fungus succeeds in spreading out of the lungs, however, it may cause serious or fatal illness requiring hospitalization. Usually, treatment is given by intravenous drip in a hospital, but it is successful in only about 40% of the cases.

Prevention: Infection provides lifelong immunity. Scientists are trying to develop a vaccine that can be given to those in high-risk regions.

Varicose veins
(VAAR-ih-kohs)

DISEASE

TYPE: MECHANICAL

See also
Bleeding and bruises
Circulatory system
Hemorrhoids
Pregnancy and disease
Thrombophlebitis
Veins

Blood is circulated to the heart from the rest of the body by a network of veins. Within each major vein is a series of valves that keep blood flowing steadily in a single direction. But sometimes the walls of the veins become stretched, so that the veins themselves become longer and wider, and the valves no longer close properly. Blood leaks backward through the valves and pools in the channels. The superficial veins nearest the skin, especially in the legs, may become swollen and twisted and appear blue or purple through the skin.

The condition may be merely unsightly, but it also may have more serious consequences. The veins may become inflamed, causing painful *phlebitis* (flih-BIY-tihs), and blood clots may then form in them, leading to potentially dangerous thrombophlebitis. Surrounding tissues may become starved for nutrients, leading to swelling, itching, pain, or ulcerous sores. Even minor injury in the area of a swollen vein may trigger hard-to-control bleeding.

Cause: The causes of varicose veins are unknown. The condition tends to run in families but is not clearly hereditary. More women than men are affected, possibly because of female hormonal influences. Both varicose veins and hemorrhoids are among the common discomforts of pregnancy. Prolonged and extreme pressure on the legs, produced by the weight of obesity or by standing immobile for long periods, may contribute to the disorder.

Incidence: Varicose veins are very common. Up to 15% of all adults and perhaps 50% of women may experience them.

Noticeable symptoms: The swellings, especially at first, are likely to be painless. These are most likely to appear in one or both of the lower legs.

Diagnosis: Diagnosis is usually based on direct observation. Special ultrasound and x-ray examinations can be used to assess the state of the veins and the functioning of the valves.

Treatment options: Varicose veins can be conservatively treated by regular exercise to stimulate circulation and control weight, by elevating the legs above the heart at intervals during the day, and by wearing elastic stockings (but otherwise avoiding tight clothes, such as girdles).

But if the condition becomes painful or complications develop, treatment to seal or remove the defective veins may become advisable. Veins can be sealed by processes such as *sclerotherapy*, in which a chemical solution is injected into the veins, causing them to close up, become scar tissue, and eventually become reabsorbed by the body. Very large varicose veins may have to be removed by surgery.

Veins

BODY SYSTEM

The veins are flexible tubes that return blood from the various parts of the body to the heart. Most veins bring the heart oxygen-poor blood, which it pumps through arteries to the lungs. From the lungs oxygen-rich blood returns through veins to the heart for pumping to the rest of the body. Lymph from the lymphatic system is also funneled into the veins.

Size and location: Veins have thinner walls than arteries, but the outside diameter is about the same. Thus the inner opening in veins is larger than in arteries. But blood does not flow as swiftly as in arteries. By the time blood has passed through the capillaries, friction has eroded the impulse from the heart. To keep the blood flowing, movements of muscles push blood

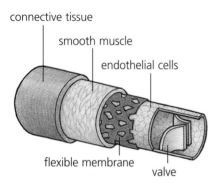

connective tissue

smooth muscle

endothelial cells

flexible membrane

valve

Veins differ physically from arteries in two main ways. The veins are thinner, reflecting less need for handling fluid pressure, and they contain many one-way valves to direct the flow of blood.

See also
Autoimmune diseases
Blood
Circulatory system
Gangrene
Hemorrhoids
Lymphatic system
Thrombophlebitis
Varicose veins

along as the muscles alternately press veins in or allow them to expand. Veins in the limbs also have one-way valves to direct the flow of blood toward the heart.

Role: Blood that is returned by the veins to the heart has lost most of its oxygen and collected waste carbon dioxide instead. Such used blood is then routed from the heart to the lungs by the pulmonary artery.

Conditions that affect the veins: Fewer difficulties arise in this low-pressure part of the circulation system than in the high-pressure, active, oxygenated heart and arteries. Failure of the valves can result in varicose veins. Varicose veins around the anus or vagina or in the lining of the rectum or colon are known as hemorrhoids. Inflammation of the lining of the veins, which may cause blood clots, is often the result of physical damage from a blow or from cutting off of circulation in a limb. This condition is called *phlebitis* or, if a clot develops in a vein as a result of an inflamed state, thrombophlebitis. *Buerger's disease,* a disease that attacks both the veins and arteries, is characterized by closure of the blood vessels from an unknown cause. In some cases it is a complication of an autoimmune disease, but it is most common among male smokers and tends to produce thrombophlebitis in the legs. If not treated, it can lead to gangrene, requiring in some cases amputation of a leg.

Venereal disease (VD)	*See* **STD (sexually transmitted diseases)**
Vertigo	*See* **Dizziness**
Vincent's disease	*See* **Trench mouth**

Viral pneumonia

DISEASE

TYPE: INFECTIOUS (VIRAL)

Pneumonia is a serious inflammation of one or both lungs. It causes the alveoli, the tiny air pockets in lungs, to fill with pus and plasma. With the lungs plugged with fluid, breathing becomes difficult. Bacteria, viruses, funguses, and chemical reactions can cause it. In most cases a person's immune system and rest can cure viral pneumonia, although other forms of pneumonia require more aggressive treatment.

Phone doctor

Get vaccinated

Cause: The most common cause of viral pneumonia in children is the respiratory syncytial (sihn-SIHSH-ee-uhl) virus. The influenza virus is a common pneumonia agent in older persons. At any age one of the adenoviruses, viruses that also produce some common colds, may induce pneumonia.

Incidence: About 15 in 1,000 Americans have pneumonia annually, and a virus is responsible for about half of all pneumonias.

Noticeable symptoms: Symptoms for any form of pneumonia include dry cough, chills, fever, shortness of breath, chest pain, and severe fatigue. As the disease progresses, the patient experiences rapid, shallow breathing, increased heart rate, profuse sweating, and bluish skin, indicating that the body is not getting enough oxygen. Infants may go into convulsions.

Anyone experiencing these symptoms should be evaluated by a physician, especially infants, people over age 65, or those who are already ill with another disease.

Diagnosis: A physician can detect the distinct breathing sounds that accompany pneumonia, examine the sputum (fluid in a cough) for the causative agent, and take x-rays of the lungs.

Treatment options: Mild cases can be treated at home, but severe cases require a hospital stay and supplemental oxygen.

Most people recover completely from viral pneumonia as a result of immune system success. But for infants under 1 year or adults over 65, whose immune systems are not so strong as those of other people, the disease can be fatal.

Prevention: For adults over 65 an annual flu shot may be effective against viral pneumonia caused by the influenza virus, although infection by a different virus can still result in the disease.

Viruses and disease

REFERENCE

In addition to mild but unpleasant diseases such as the common cold and gastroenteritis, viruses can cause life-threatening diseases and some serious epidemics. As a result most people suffer at least one viral disease annually, and millions die from viral disease each year. Until recently, the main defenses against viral diseases were prevention and rest, for once a viral disease started, there was no effective medication to treat it.

The nature of viruses: Most viruses consist of a strand or two of genetic material (the genome, which is DNA or, in some viruses, the related molecule RNA) along with a protein *envelope* (sometimes called a *coat*) to enclose the genetic material. A virus uses its genetic material to take over part of a living cell, which it then directs to produce more copies of itself.

How viruses travel: Different viruses can remain infective in different situations. Some, such as the viruses that cause the common cold, maintain their integrity on solid surfaces. The virus that causes hepatitis A remains infective in water. Other viruses, such as that for influenza, remain infective in droplets expelled with a cough. The herpes viruses may require one person to touch another for the disease to be transmitted. Some, such as the HIV virus that causes AIDS or the hepatitis B virus, will not pass from one person to another unless certain bodily fluids, such as blood or semen, carry it.

Some viruses normally live in more than one species, perhaps causing a disease in one while sparing the other host. The *arboviruses* live in insects and other arthropods, such as ticks and mites. They cause such diseases in humans as encephalitis and hemorrhagic fevers. The *hantaviruses* live in rodents, but also cause hemorrhagic fevers in humans.

How a virus causes disease: Although the main purpose of a virus is to produce more copies of itself, it has to get into the interior of a cell and often into the nucleus of the cell to achieve that goal. First, the virus must attach itself to a suitable cell; it does this by being grabbed by a cell protein that

A virus reproduces by taking over part of the DNA in a cell and subverting it to manufacture more copies of itself. These copies eventually make the interior of the cell more acid. The acidity releases a spring mechanism that pushes the copies out of the cell, where they then latch onto receptors on other cells and begin the process anew.

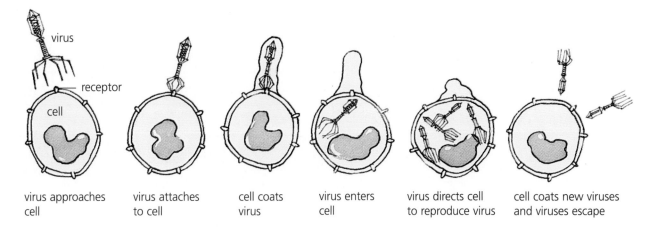

virus approaches cell

virus attaches to cell

cell coats virus

virus enters cell

virus directs cell to reproduce virus

cell coats new viruses and viruses escape

protrudes through the cell membrane. This protein is called a *receptor*. Receptor molecules normally bring specific proteins or other chemicals through the cell membrane and into the cell for the cell's own uses. Some viruses have parts of their outer envelope that resemble molecules that a receptor is intended to grab; as a result a receptor takes hold of a virus as the germ passes the cell, wraps the virus in a bit of cell membrane, and pulls the package into the interior of the cell. Other viruses have their own mechanisms for attaching to a cell's outer membrane.

Frequently, viruses affect the body in ways that alter the mode in which the body works, often causing permanent damage.

Cell damage or death: Often cells infected by viruses are damaged and fail to work properly. In some cases the cells die after they have helped the virus reproduce.

Immune response: Many of the symptoms associated with viral diseases are actually part of the immune system's methods for ridding the body of the virus—such effects range from runny noses to fevers. These effects of viral infection are usually not themselves harmful to the person with the disease, but they are often unpleasant. In some cases a response such as fever can reach a level that is fatal.

Cancer: After the workings of DNA began to be unraveled in the 1950s and 1960s, it became apparent that since viruses modify DNA, they have the power to cause cancer, which is essentially a disease of DNA. Viruses are known to have a role in producing warts that are often precursors of cancer (the human papillomaviruses). Herpes viruses may also cause cancer, perhaps in interactions with papillomaviruses. The hepatitis B virus is thought to promote liver cancer.

Autoimmune diseases: Viruses are strongly suspected of initiating the attacks by the immune system on a person's tissue that are known as autoimmune diseases. One example is diabetes mellitus type I, in which the immune system attacks the insulin-producing cells of the pancreas.

Prevention and treatment: Vaccines encourage the immune system to produce chemicals called antibodies that are specific to a particular virus. Vaccines have been developed for many viral diseases, including the vaccine for rabies, which was among the

Some families of viruses

Virus family	Typical diseases	Typical symptoms
Adenoviruses	Tonsillitis, some instances of the common cold	Sore throat, flulike symptoms
Arboviruses	Encephalitis, dengue fever, yellow fever, Rift Valley fever	Brain inflammation, hemorrhage
Arenaviruses	Lassa fever, meningitis	Brain inflammation, hemorrhage
Coronaviruses	Common cold	Nasal congestion
Cytomegaloviruses	Cytomegalovirus infection (opportunistic)	Damage to newborns
Enteroviruses	Poliomyelitis, hepatitis A	Nerve inflammation, diarrhea
Filoviruses	Ebola, Marburg	Hemorrhage, diarrhea
Hantaviruses	Hantavirus pulmonary syndrome, Hantaan fever	Hemorrhage, fever, fluid-filled lungs
Herpesviruses	Chicken pox, mononucleosis, shingles, cold sores, genital herpes	Nerve damage, sores and pustules
Influenza viruses	Influenza	Respiratory distress, cough, fever
Papillomaviruses	Warts, cancer	Bumps on skin or mucous membranes
Parainfluenza and RSV viruses	RSV (respiratory syncytial virus), bronchitis, croup, viral pneumonia	Cough, inflammation of lungs
Paramyxoviruses	Measles, mumps,	Respiratory inflammation
Retroviruses	AIDS, leukemia	Immune deficiencies
Rhinoviruses	Common cold	Runny nose and cough
Rotaviruses	Gastroenteritis	Diarrhea

first to be produced. More recently, scientists have been able to locate the part of a virus that stimulates the immune system to attack it; they then use genetic engineering to produce that part as a vaccine.

"Virus" infection

DISEASE

TYPE: INFECTIOUS (VIRAL)

You have not felt well for several days, so you visit a healthcare worker. You are informed: "It's just that virus that's going around. Get some rest, and you'll be better in a day or two." No drugs prescribed. No blood tests. No cultures taken. What's going on?

No drugs are prescribed against a "virus" infection because almost no drugs are effective against viral agents. A blood test could reveal antibodies to a specific virus if some well-known virus was the cause, but little is known about many mild viral diseases. No cultures are taken partly because of the impossibility of growing a virus except in living cells.

Cause: Most unspecified virus infections are either of the type that causes flulike symptoms or of the type that causes stomach upset and diarrhea. The first of these infections, in the absence of the runny nose and congestion of the common cold, is usually called *summer flu,* although the disease is not likely to be influenza except during the winter, when influenza is epidemic. The second, officially known as viral gastroenteritis, is probably caused by a virus that can live for a time in water or food and that affects the lining of the digestive system.

The symptoms of infection by several hundred different viruses are so similar because most symptoms are caused by the immune response to the virus, not by something that the virus itself does. In more serious viral diseases the virus damages and perhaps kills cells. But the mild unspecified virus infections provoke a response without causing much damage.

Incidence: Unspecified virus diseases are so common that nearly everyone has one or more episodes each year.

Noticeable symptoms: Flulike symptoms caused by the immune response are fever, chills, headache, overall fatigue, and a feeling of sickness. Often you know that something is wrong with the way you feel but have trouble pinning it down. If the virus affects the digestive system, there may also be nausea or diarrhea or both.

Diagnosis: There may be redness in the throat or a rash that can be observed as well as a rise in temperature that can be measured. The main thing that a physician will want to establish is that the disease is not caused by a bacterium, which would be more serious if left untreated, and which could probably be treated by antibiotics.

Treatment options: If the illness is a mild viral infection, there is little to be done but rest, drink plenty of liquids, perhaps take an acetaminophen pill for headache or pain relief—and wait. The ill feeling is caused by the body trying to rid itself of the virus, which it is nearly always successful in doing.

Wash hands

Prevention: Viral diseases spread from person to person in many cases, with the virus often carried on hard surfaces such as table utensils. Be careful about what you touch if someone with a viral disease is in the household, at school, or at the office. Always wash your hands after going to the bathroom. Some viruses spread in coughs or sneezes, so maintain a safe distance from a person exhibiting these symptoms. Still, it is difficult to avoid catching such diseases from time to time.

Vitamin-deficiency diseases

Humans require only small amounts of vitamins, but these are essential for maintaining vital body processes. Several conditions recognized as diseases occur when vitamins are missing from the diet. Some vitamins, such as A, D, and E, are *fat-soluble,* while those that the body eliminates rapidly, such as B vitamins, C, and K, are *water-soluble.* A balanced diet should include foods with all the vitamins each day.

Vitamins and health: The reason that the body needs vitamins is that, with the exception of vitamin D and niacin, which are not true vitamins, the body cannot manufacture these chemicals and must obtain them from food. Often animals other than humans are able to manufacture vitamins that humans cannot—primates and hamsters are the only mammals that cannot make their own vitamin C, for example. Plants also can produce these compounds. Since these compounds are necessary for life, it is presumed that they were all a regular part of the diet of human ancestors and that we save energy by not making them in our own bodies. When the modern diet does not come up to that of our ancestors, we need to take vitamin supplements.

Here is a summary of the main vitamins needed for health.

- *Vitamin A:* Also called *retinol* (REHT-n-awl), this vitamin is important for maintaining healthy skin and other body tissues, for proper wound healing, and for normal functioning of the eyes. Vitamin A deficiency is common among the elderly, the urban poor, people who abuse laxatives, and alcoholics. One of the early symptoms is *night blindness,* the inability to see in dim light. Vitamin A is poisonous in

The Food Pyramid
Many vitamins are found in the grains, fruits, and vegetables in the wide lower bands of the Food Pyramid, but some occur only in the dairy products, meats, and fats that are near the top. The pyramid is intended to show that you need smaller amounts of the foods in the upper levels than you do of the foods in the lower levels; you are not supposed to eliminate foods from upper levels entirely, since you need the vitamins that are found only there.

large doses. It builds up in fat tissues, so it is good to keep close to recommended amounts.

- *Vitamin B₁:* Also called *thiamine* (THIY-uh-mihn), B_1 is important in the process of breaking down carbohydrates and also affects the functioning of nerves. Thiamine deficiency—*beriberi*—is most commonly seen in chronic alcoholics. Beriberi usually begins with mild symptoms, including muscle cramps, irritability, loss of appetite, and prickling or burning sensations in the skin. As the disease advances, it may affect either the heart or the nervous system. Without treatment death may result from heart failure or paralysis. People with diets heavy in highly refined grains, with chronic diarrhea or intestinal absorption problems, and on dialysis may also develop thiamine deficiency.

Thiamine is one of a group known as B-complex vitamins. B-complex vitamins usually occur together in foods, so symptoms of deficiency disorders for several B vitamins often appear simultaneously.

- *Vitamin B₂:* Also called *riboflavin* (RIY-boh-FLAY-vihn), this vitamin figures in the body's oxidation processes and is also a key component in certain enzymes. Riboflavin deficiency is among the most common deficiency disorders in the United States and usually appears along with deficiencies of other vitamins. The symptoms are comparatively mild, including anemia, mouth and lip sores, skin problems, and eye problems.

- *Niacin:* Another of the B vitamins, niacin figures in the body's oxidation processes. The body can synthesize it from the amino acid tryptophan, so it is not a true vitamin. Niacin deficiency is called pellagra; once common in the southern United States, it is now often seen in chronic alcoholics and drug addicts. Severe cases include three basic symptoms—diarrhea, skin problems, and dementia or learning difficulties. Advanced pellagra can cause death.

- *Vitamin B₆:* This vitamin is actually a group of substances that play a role in metabolism. Chronic alcoholism and interactions of certain medications, including oral contraceptives, can cause deficiency disorders of B_6. Mouth soreness, irritability, and weakness are among the early symptoms, while anemia, seizures, and other symptoms appear in advanced cases.

- *Vitamin B₁₂:* This vitamin is a factor in the production of red blood cells. Vitamin B_{12} deficiency is called *pernicious anemia* and usually appears in the elderly because the small intestine is failing to absorb the vitamin. Numbness in the hands and feet, sore tongue, weight loss, weakness, and rapid heartbeat are among the symptoms of this disease. Left untreated the deficiency can eventually cause death. Vitamin B_{12} is not found in vegetables, so strict vegetarians need to supplement their diet in some way.

- *Vitamin C:* Also called *ascorbic acid,* it helps maintain healthy connective tissue, cartilage, and bone, and is involved in metabolism. The elderly, who may neglect their diet, people who are too poor to feed themselves properly, and alcoholics are among those who may contract the vitamin C deficiency disease called scurvy. The early symptoms of scurvy include swollen gums, loose teeth, and small black-and-blue spots on the skin. Untreated, scurvy leads to a decline in health and eventually death.

- *Vitamin D:* This vitamin is involved in calcium and phosphorus absorption by the body. When exposed to sunlight, the skin manufactures vitamin D, making it not a true vitamin. Vitamin D deficiency in children is called rickets; in adults, osteomalacia. The deficiency results in the body not having enough calcium to maintain healthy bone structure and leads to softening of bones and serious bone deformities.

- *Vitamin E:* Vitamin E is an antioxidant that can protect cell structures from damage by highly reactive groups of atoms in the body called free radicals. It may also help protect against cancer, cataracts, and heart disease. Vitamin E deficiency is usually due to problems with absorption by the intestines. It causes difficulty with walking, poor reflexes, short stature, and paralysis of eye muscles.

- *Vitamin K:* Actually a group of substances, vitamin K helps promote clotting of blood. A deficiency may occur fairly quickly because the body stores so little vitamin K. The disorder may result from poor diet or failure of the intestines to absorb the vitamin, or when antibiotics administered for other medical reasons kill off bacteria that normally live in the intestines and that synthesize the vitamin. As the deficiency develops, the patient experiences bruising and bleeding that is difficult to stop.

The best way to get the vitamins you need is from a healthy diet. This should include several daily servings of fortified whole grain cereals for B vitamins, vitamin E, and folic acid; fruit for vitamins A and C; and fortified milk for vitamins A and D. Peanut butter is rich in thiamine and niacin.

- *Folic acid:* Also known as *folacin* or *folate,* folic acid is needed to prevent anemia and may help protect against heart attack. It also is needed by pregnant women to help prevent neural tube defects in the fetus.
- *Biotin* (BIY-uh-tihn)*:* Found in meat, whole grains, and nuts, biotin is involved in processing proteins, carbohydrates, and fats. Lack of it causes skin problems, nausea, and depression.
- *Pantothenic acid:* Found in organ meats such as liver, most vegetables, eggs, and whole grains, pantothenic acid is involved with the production of neurotransmitters and hormones. The principal symptom for those few who develop a deficiency is fatigue and sometimes burning feet.

Selected vitamins and their food sources

Vitamin	Deficiency disease	Food sources of vitamin
A	Night blindness	Eggs, whole milk, cream, butter, cheese, liver, green and yellow vegetables (carrots, squash, sweet potatoes, spinach, kale, and broccoli)
B_1 (thiamine)	Beriberi	Ham, pork, milk, fortified cereals, peanuts, liver, raisins, soybeans, seafood
B_2 (riboflavin)	Poor growth, skin disorders, sensitivity to light (ariboflavinosis)	Liver, beef, ham, milk, green vegetables, fortified cereals, yeast
Niacin	Pellagra	Peanuts, lean meats, poultry, fish, bran, yeast, liver
B_6	Skin disorders, anemia, convulsions	Whole-grain cereals, fish, legumes, liver and other organ meats, yeast
B_{12}	Pernicious anemia	Eggs, milk, liver, beef, poultry, shellfish
C (ascorbic acid)	Scurvy	Fresh fruits, such as oranges and other citrus fruits; fresh vegetables, such as Brussels sprouts and cabbage
D	Rickets, osteomalacia	Fortified milk, saltwater fish, egg yolks, fish liver oil
E	Impaired reproduction; weakened muscles	Vegetable seed oil, cereals, beef, liver, cheese, milk, shellfish, cabbage
K	Bleeding, poor clot formation	Leafy green vegetables, dairy products
Folic acid	Slowed growth, anemia	Oranges, liver, chicken, beans, peas, peanuts, yeast, dark green and leafy vegetables (such as spinach or kale), wheat germ, bran
Biotin	Skin disorders, muscle paralysis, hair loss	Meats, egg yolk, oats, nuts and seeds, brown rice, peas and beans

Vomiting	*See* **Nausea**

von Willebrand's disease

(WIHL-uh-braandz)

DISEASE

TYPE: GENETIC

See also
Blood
Genetic diseases
Hemophilias

Von Willebrand's disease is a relatively common inherited disorder that can interfere with normal blood clotting. In consequence, minor wounds or surgery—even dental work—may cause excessive external or internal bleeding.

Cause: The disease results from a deficiency or abnormality in a protein called the von Willebrand factor, which is needed to facilitate the first stage of blood clotting: the concentration, or aggregation, of small, flat bodies called platelets at the site of a wound. Platelets release chemical substances necessary for the formation of clots, and if there are not enough of them at the site, clots will form slowly or not at all.

The defects in von Willebrand factor are caused by mutations in a dominant gene; that is, it can be inherited from just one parent who also has the gene and who also has the disease, although it may be too mild to be recognized.

Incidence: Von Willebrand's disease is believed to be quite common—possibly affecting 1 in 100 individuals. Many of these are so little affected, however, that they may not know that they have it.

Noticeable symptoms: Excessive bleeding from small cuts and unusual susceptibility to bruising may become noticeable as early as infancy or early childhood.

Diagnosis: Blood tests of factor activity and DNA analysis can be used to identify affected individuals and their parents.

Treatment: Von Willebrand's disease is customarily treated with a synthetic pituitary hormone called desmopressin, administered in a nasal spray. It causes the von Willebrand factor to be released from body cells into the blood plasma and can raise the level high enough to restore normal function.

People with von Willebrand's disease should avoid certain drugs that aggravate bleeding. These include blood thinners such as heparin and warfarin and painkillers such as aspirin and ibuprofen.

Avoid aspirin

Walleye

See **Crossed eyes; Eyes and vision**

Warts

DISEASE

TYPE: INFECTIOUS (VIRAL)

See also
Cancers
Foot problems
STD (sexually transmitted diseases)

Warts, or *verrucas* (vuh-ROO-kuhs), are small lumps on the surface of the skin that look and sometimes feel unpleasant but usually are nothing more than a nuisance. Caused by a virus that establishes itself in tiny breaks in the skin, common warts usually are only somewhat contagious. The exception is *genital warts,* which are highly contagious and are spread through sexual contact. Babies may contract the warts from their mother during birth.

Size and location: Most warts are smaller than a pea. Warts can appear anywhere on the body. Most grow on the hands, feet, elbows, knees, scalp, and face. Although sometimes skin colored, they are often darker or lighter or sometimes even tan or pink.

Warts that grow on the bottom of the foot are usually called *plantar* (PLAAN-tuhr) *warts.* Unlike other warts these may be sensitive to pressure and may make walking uncomfortable. *Senile warts* are those that appear on older people, and *soft warts* may appear on the eyelids, ears, or neck of people who work with hydrocarbons. *Venereal* (vuh-NEER-ee-uhl) *warts,* also called *genital warts,* can appear on a man's penis, in a woman's vagina, and in the anus.

Cause: Various strains of human papillomavirus (HPV) cause warts. Once HPV enters the body it causes skin cells in the immediate area to multiply rapidly. The result is a fibrous lump of tissue that pushes up out of the skin's surface.

Incidence: Warts are common in children, especially teenagers, and millions of people seek treatment for them each year. Adults get ordinary warts much less frequently (about 30% of all cases treated), possibly because they have developed an immunity to HPV.

People who are over 45 and develop what appears to be a wart should get medical attention. The growth could be skin cancer or another serious skin condition.

Venereal warts are relatively common among adults. Pregnant women tend to get venereal warts because HPV travels in moisture, and the vagina is wetter than usual during pregnancy. Women who get venereal warts have a higher risk of developing cervical cancer; there are also increased cancer risks for men from genital warts.

Noticeable symptoms: Warts are small, round lumps of hard flesh. Except on the soles of the feet, where they are subject to pressure, they usually protrude slightly above the skin; their tops have a cauliflowerlike appearance. Deeper inside plantar warts are black streaks or flecks that are clotted blood vessels.

Treatment options: Common warts can be removed by a number of means. Nonprescription remedies, including plasters, lotions, and ointments, destroy the abnormal tissue of the wart by chemical action. These preparations should not be used on the face or on venereal warts, where skin is more sensitive.

When nonprescription remedies fail, or when venereal warts are present, a physician may prescribe a stronger medication such as a catalytic agent or may freeze the wart with liquid nitrogen. Other methods include burning warts off with electricity or lasers or surgical removal.

Stages and progress: Normally, it takes between one and eight months after infection for a wart to develop. Though some persist for years without treatment, warts often disappear on their own.

Prevention: Avoid scratching, rubbing, or cutting a wart with a razor because this can spread the virus to a new site.

Myths about warts

Because most warts seem to come and go somewhat mysteriously, they have inspired origin myths and some strange home remedies. For example, the popular idea that touching a toad or a frog can give you warts has as its basis that toads appear warty themselves. Mark Twain reported a Missouri cure for warts—wash them in stagnant water from a tree stump. A home remedy used for warts during the 1800s was to grind dried ivy leaves to a powder, wet the wart with strong vinegar, sprinkle on the powder, and bind with a strip of rag. Such remedies often seemed to work, since warts sometimes just go away. In the 1980s methods of culturing wart-causing viruses in the laboratory were finally perfected. Researchers have identified over 67 strains of HPV and clearly established warts as a virus infection.

West Nile virus

In the fall of 1999 people in New York State began to fall ill with serious symptoms of viral infection and inflammation of the brain (encephalitis). What was first thought to be St. Louis encephalitis—a familiar but unwelcome disease in the eastern United States—turned out to be West Nile encephalitis, a disease never before seen in the western hemisphere.

Cause: West Nile encephalitis is caused by West Nile virus (WNV). It is transmitted to humans by the bite of an infected mosquito. The mosquitoes get infected by biting an infected bird, usually a crow or bluejay.

In 1999, 62 people became seriously ill with WNV infection, and 8 died. But a follow-up study showed that more than 1,300 New Yorkers had actually been infected. Most people with WNV have such mild symptoms that they do not seek medical care.

Noticeable symptoms: Mild symptoms of WNV infection include fever, body aches, rash, and swollen glands. More severe symptoms include high fever, stiff neck, severe headache, disorientation, tremors, muscle weakness, and convulsions.

Diagnosis: A doctor will ask about mosquito bites and can do a blood test to determine if there is a WNV infection.

Treatment: Like most viral diseases there is no cure but allowing the immune system to rid the body of the virus. In the case of severe symptoms, however, the patient is hospitalized, and intensive supportive treatment such as fluids and breathing assistance are provided while the patient's body fights the virus.

Prevention: Avoiding mosquitoes is the single best prevention for WNV infection. Eliminate standing water where mosquitoes breed, wear long pants and long-sleeved shirts, use insect repellent, and stay inside when mosquitoes are active.

Whiplash

INJURY

Whiplash is an injury of the neck that can cause considerable discomfort. It may be a sign of serious injury. Whiplash typically happens in an auto accident when the head of the driver or passenger is thrown violently forward and backward by the force of the crash. The sharp movements damage muscles and

Whiplash was once a common result of even minor auto accidents, especially rear-end collisions. New cars with raised headrests have reduced the incidence of the injury. Better seat belts, and laws mandating wearing them while driving or riding, have also decreased both the number and severity of injuries from automobile accidents.

ligaments connecting bones in the upper part of the spinal column and may even cause a ruptured disk.

Closely related to this disorder is shaken baby syndrome, in which injuries are caused by violently shaking a child who is under three years of age.

Cause: Pain from injuries sustained in an auto accident may result from pressure on nerves in the neck. A ruptured disk may also cause pain by putting pressure on nerves. At other times there may be no apparent injury causing the pain.

Incidence: Whiplash is suffered by about 20% of people involved in rear-end auto collisions.

Noticeable symptoms: There may be brief loss of consciousness. Afterward there may be pain and muscle spasms in the back of the neck. A headache and stiff shoulders and neck are common.

Diagnosis: Damage to the neck in less serious cases of whiplash usually does not show on x-rays. In more severe cases the patient may have a ruptured disk or fractured vertebra.

Treatment options: Mild pain medications, heat, massage, and perhaps a padded collar to reduce neck movement may be all that is necessary for mild whiplash.

Prevention: Using raised headrests in a car helps prevent whiplash in the front vehicle of a rear-end collision. Wearing a seat belt across both the waist and chest prevents the head from snapping forward so far it hits the dashboard or window when the car collides with another or with a stationery object.

Whipworm

DISEASE

TYPE: PARASITIC

Small cylindrical worms with whiplike tails may take up residence in a person's large intestine, where they may live for years without causing symptoms.

Cause: Whipworm infection, also called *trichuriasis* (TRIHK-yuh-RIY-uh-sihs), is caused by *Trichuris trichiura*. This parasite is about one to two inches long. People become infected by accidentally eating the eggs, either on contaminated food or passed into the mouth from improperly washed hands before eating.

Wash hands

Incidence: An estimated 800 million people are infected worldwide. Infections are most common in warm, moist tropical and subtropical areas, particularly in places with poor sanitation.

Noticeable symptoms: Most whipworm infections are light and do not cause symptoms. Heavy infestations cause bloody diarrhea and abdominal pain. There may be anemia from loss of blood.

Diagnosis: If a physician suspects whipworm, your stool will be examined for eggs.

Treatment options: Whipworms can be killed with the antiworm medication mebendazole, taken orally.

Prevention: Adequate sanitation and good personal hygiene can prevent infections.

White blood cells

See **Lymphocytes; Phagocytes and other leukocytes**

Whooping cough

See **Pertussis**

Wilms tumor

DISEASE

TYPE: CANCER; GENETIC

Cancer in children is rare. One of the more common kinds is a cancer of the kidney called Wilms tumor. It usually appears in children under five and most often occurs in just one kidney, but in about 4% of cases it affects both.

Cause: The disease appears to be at least partly genetic, but usually, like many cancers, the exact cause is unknown.

Incidence: Wilms tumor occurs in about 1 in 200,000 births and is observed most often around age three.

Noticeable symptoms: Usually, the first noticeable sign of the tumor is a firm mass that can be felt in the abdomen or lower back. Other symptoms may include abdominal pain, fever, nausea, loss of appetite, and blood in the urine.

Diagnosis: Diagnosis is usually based on physical examination confirmed by imaging techniques such as ultrasound, x-ray using injected dye, computed tomography (CT), or magnetic resonance imaging (MRI). A tissue sample, or biopsy, is usually collected to determine the nature of the malignant cells.

Treatment options: Like other cancers Wilms tumor is treated with surgery, chemotherapy, and radiation.

Outlook: Wilms tumor can be successfully treated in most children, especially if it occurs in just one kidney and has not spread to other tissues and organs.

Wilson's disease

DISEASE

TYPE: GENETIC

See also
Anemias
Diet and disease
Genetic diseases
Jaundice
Mental illnesses

Copper is found in small amounts in the body and is needed for several normal functions. Normally any excess copper is processed by the liver and excreted in bile. In the inherited birth defect known as Wilson's disease copper builds up and progressively damages the liver, brain, and other organs.

Cause: An abnormal gene on chromosome 13 produces a faulty molecule, one that normally controls the distribution of copper within the body. The pattern of inheritance is recessive.

Incidence: Wilson's disease is relatively uncommon—about 1 in 30,000 persons worldwide, or more than 9,000 Americans, have the disorder.

Noticeable symptoms: The condition appears most frequently during late adolescence.

The first symptoms are often like those of viral hepatitis, including jaundice, fatigue and weakness, nausea and loss of appetite, and abdominal swelling and pain. There may also be effects on the brain: tremors, difficulties with walking and talking, depression, and irritability.

Diagnosis: The disease can generally be diagnosed by a series of blood and urine tests or, if necessary, by a liver biopsy. An eye examination may reveal a rusty brown ring in the cornea of the eye.

Treatment options: Treatment for Wilson's disease halts the damage from copper poisoning but does not cure the disorder. For the rest of their lives those affected must take drugs called *chelators* (KEE-lay-tuhrs), which bind the excessive copper in the system and allow it to be excreted in urine. Chelators may be supplemented by zinc acetate, which blocks copper from being absorbed through the intestines into the blood. It may be helpful to follow a low-copper diet, avoiding shellfish and liver.

If the liver has become severely damaged, a liver transplant may be needed.

Outlook: Wilson's disease is progressive and eventually fatal if not diagnosed and treated. When treatment begins early enough and continues without interruption, patients can live healthy, normal lives.

Damage to the liver and other organs may occur before any symptoms appear. It is advisable for family members of patients with Wilson's disease to be tested to find out if they are also affected, even if they seem to be in good health.

Womb

See **Uterus**

Xanthoma

See **Skin diseases**

Yaws
(YAWZ)

DISEASE

TYPE: INFECTIOUS (BACTERIAL)

A red sore that looks somewhat like a raspberry, with many little granules, may be the first sign of the tropical disease yaws, also known as *frambesia* (fraam-BEE-zhuh) *tropica*. Left untreated, this disease can destroy large areas of a person's skin and bones.

Cause: Yaws is caused by a spiral-shaped bacterium, *Treponema pertenue*. (It is so closely related to the bacterium that causes syphilis that some bacteriologists consider *T. pertenue* to be a subspecies of the syphilis bacterium.) Yaws is highly infectious. It is transmitted from one person to another by direct contact.

Incidence: Yaws is found in warm, humid parts of the tropics and subtropics, especially in poor areas that lack proper sanitation. It is most common among young children.

See also
Bacteria and disease
Syphilis
Tropical diseases

Noticeable symptoms: In the first stage of the disease an ulcerating sore—the "mother yaw"—appears at the point where the bacterium entered the body. This sore is itchy and very infectious. Scratching spreads the infection to other parts of the body. Touching someone with the scratching hand spreads the infection to that person. Soon the mother yaw recedes, but new sores appear at various places on the body.

Diagnosis: Initial diagnosis is based on the unique appearance of the sores. Samples taken from the sores will be examined for *Treponema* bacteria.

Treatment options: Yaws is treated with the antibiotic penicillin. A single massive dose is sufficient to cure it.

Stages and progress: The first stage of the infection is visible about three to four weeks after infection. The mother yaw appears, grows larger, and develops a crust. Then it disappears, leaving a scar.

The second stage appears weeks or even months after the first stage disappears. It is marked by many red pimples all over the body but especially on the face, arms, legs, and buttocks. These, too, become ulcerous.

Left untreated, there is a third stage when yaws can result in widespread tissue loss. The disease destroys large areas of skin and bone and causes a shortening of the fingers or toes.

Prevention: A program of treatment of whole villages with antibiotics has greatly reduced incidence of this disease, which was once widespread in tropical regions around the world.

Yeast infection

See **Candidiasis**

Yellow fever

DISEASE

TYPE: INFECTIOUS (VIRAL)

Yellow fever brings a high fever and a yellowish tinge to the patient's skin because the liver is usually affected.

Cause: Yellow fever is caused by a virus. In the United States and most other places yellow fever is transmitted by bites from *Aedes aegypti* mosquitoes. These mosquitoes tend to breed around cities and other places where large numbers of people live, but they also inhabit tropical rain forests where monkeys are present. The yellow fever virus can be transmitted by mosquitoes from monkey to monkey, forming a reservoir for the disease.

Incidence: Though yellow fever is virtually nonexistent in the United States and many other parts of the world, outbreaks still occur, primarily in parts of Africa and South America.

Today there are about 200,000 new cases of yellow fever annually around the world, causing 30,000 deaths each year.

Noticeable symptoms: Yellow fever starts abruptly with headache, muscle aches, backache, and fever. A break in the fever occurs after about three days, but in one case out of seven it returns. Along with the fever come delirium, jaundice, slowed heartbeat, vomiting (with blood), and bleeding from the mucous membranes. The name "yellow fever" comes from the jaundice phase.

Diagnosis: In diagnosing yellow fever a doctor must first rule out other diseases that cause similar symptoms, including hepatitis, malaria, and dengue. A sophisticated blood test is needed to confirm the diagnosis.

Treatment options: There is no cure for yellow fever. Instead doctors try to control the symptoms while the disease runs its course.

Prevention: The principal tool is a highly effective vaccine. People traveling to areas where yellow fever is still a problem, such as tropical rain forests inhabited by monkeys, should get vaccinated. Where outbreaks occur in urban areas, campaigns to eliminate mosquitoes are generally successful in stopping the disease.

Get vaccinated

Zoonoses

See **Animal diseases and humans; Pets and disease**

INDEX

A

Abdominal wall defects **2**:99
Abruptio placentae **7**:5, **7**:10, **7**:14
Abscess **1**:9–10, **2**:16–17, **7**:35
Acetaminophen **6**:58
Achalasia **2**:56, **3**:102
Achilles tendon **8**:67–68
Achlorhydria **8**:22
Achondroplasia **4**:104, **7**:84–85
Acid reflux **4**:40
Acne **1**:10–12
Acoustic neuroma **3**:52, **8**:85
Acromegaly **4**:104, **6**:99
ACTH (adrenocorticotropic hormone) **4**:102
Actinomycetes **1**:97
Acupuncture **6**:59
Acute inflammatory polyneuropathy. *See* Guillain-Barré syndrome
Acute lymphocytic leukemia **5**:56
Acute nonlymphocytic leukemia **5**:56
Acute porphyrias **7**:3–4
Acute pyelonephritis **5**:36
Acyclovir **2**:88, **4**:36
ADA deficiency **1**:12–13, **5**:3
Addiction **3**:57, **3**:59–60
Addison, Thomas **4**:106
Addison's disease **1**:17, **1**:91, **4**:104, **4**:106, **8**:22
Adenine **4**:38
Adenoids **6**:26, **8**:62
Adenoma **8**:85
Adenomyosis **3**:90
Adenosine deaminase. *See* ADA deficiency
Adenoviruses **1**:87, **8**:103
ADH (antidiuretic hormone) **3**:29, **4**:103, **6**:98
Adrenal glands **1**:16–17, **3**:89, **6**:77–78
ADHD (attention-deficit/hyperactivity disorder) **1**:13–15
Adrenaline. *See* Epinephrine
Adult acne. *See* Rosacea
Aedes aegypti (mosquito) **3**:20
African sleeping sickness **6**:72
Afterbirth. *See* Placenta
Agent Orange **2**:66
Agoraphobia **6**:63

Agranulocytes **6**:92
Agranulocytosis **6**:24
AIDS (acquired immunodeficiency syndrome) **1**:17–22, **8**:13, **8**:15–16
  and blood transfusions **1**:46
  entry through birth canal **1**:109
  history **1**:21
  HIV testing **1**:19
  and immune system **5**:4, **5**:5
  as modern pandemic **3**:98
  opportunistic diseases **6**:39–40
  Pneumocystis carinii **1**:20, **6**:105–6
AIDS dementia **1**:20
Air sac **5**:66
Albinism **1**:22–24, **7**:104
Alcohol
  and cancer **2**:35
  fetal alcohol syndrome **1**:28, **3**:116–17
  and frostbite **4**:19–20
  nausea from **6**:14
Alcoholics Anonymous **1**:25, **1**:27, **5**:100
Alcoholism **1**:24–29
  alcoholic siderosis **7**:88
  and cirrhosis of the liver **2**:75
  delirium tremens **1**:25, **3**:16–17
  dementia **3**:19–20
  Korsakoff's syndrome **1**:42
  pancreatitis **6**:62–63
  paranoia **6**:68
Alcohol poisoning **1**:24
ALD (adrenoleukodystrophy) **1**:29–30
Aldosterone **1**:16, **4**:102
Allele **4**:39
Allergens **1**:30–34, **1**:74, **4**:60
Allergic contact dermatitis **7**:32
Allergic purpura **7**:26
Allergic rhinitis. *See* Hay fever
Allergies **1**:30–34
  from animals **6**:89
  asthma **1**:73–77
  hay fever **1**:31, **4**:60–62
  and immune system **5**:3

and itching **5**:26
  to stings **8**:20, **8**:21
Allodynia **7**:80
Alper, Tikva **7**:16
Alpha interferon **4**:90
ALS (amyotrophic lateral sclerosis) **1**:34–37, **6**:65
Altitude sickness. *See* Polycythemia
Alveoli **2**:109, **3**:82–83, **5**:66, **7**:39
Alzheimer's disease **1**:37–40
  dementia **3**:19–20
Amblyopia **3**:106–7
Amebic dysentery **1**:9, **3**:60–62, **6**:72
Amenorrhea **1**:40–41
Amino acids **4**:39
Amnesia **1**:41–43, **2**:96
Amniocentesis **2**:70
Amniotic fluid **3**:117, **7**:12–13
Amphetamines **3**:58
Amyloidosis **8**:31–32
Amyotrophic lateral sclerosis. *See* ALS
Analgesia **7**:78
Anal itching **5**:26
Anaphylactic shock **1**:32, **7**:83, **8**:31
Anaphylaxis **5**:44
Anemia(s) **1**:43–47, **3**:114
  aplastic **1**:44
  pernicious **1**:44, **8**:22
  in pregnancy **7**:9
  thalassemia **1**:44, **8**:46–47
  See also Sickle cell anemia
Anencephaly **6**:22
Anesthetics, local **6**:59
Aneurysm **1**:47–49, **2**:75, **5**:25, **8**:27
Angina **1**:50–51, **2**:40
Angiography **1**:79, **3**:75–76
Angioplasty **1**:80, **4**:79
Angiotensin **3**:33
Angle-closure glaucoma **4**:47
Animal bites **1**:54, **6**:91
  snakebites **7**:112–14
  spider bites **8**:1–2
Animal diseases and humans **1**:51–55
  anthrax **1**:54, **1**:58–61
  cryptosporidiosis **3**:4–5
  Q fever **7**:27–28
  rabies **1**:51, **1**:53, **6**:89, **7**:29–30

tularemia **8**:84
  See also Pets and disease
Animal models **1**:54
Ankylosing spondylitis **1**:93, **1**:95
Anopheles mosquito **5**:80
Anorexia nervosa **1**:55–58
Anosmia **6**:26–27, **7**:78
Ant **8**:20
Antegrade amnesia **1**:41
Anterior compartment syndrome **4**:17
Anthracosis **3**:94
Anthrax **1**:54, **1**:58–61
  bioterrorism **3**:81
Antibiotics
  for gonorrhea **4**:49
  for infants **5**:9
Antibodies **5**:2–3, **5**:75, **6**:92–93
  in rheumatoid arthritis **7**:46
Anticoagulants **3**:76
Anticonvulsants **3**:100, **6**:58
Antidepressants **6**:58
Antidiuretic hormone. *See* ADH
Antigens **1**:32
Antihistamines **4**:61–62, **4**:99
Anti-inflammatory drugs **6**:58
Antipsychotic drugs **7**:68–69
Antiretrovirals **1**:19
Antivenin **7**:113
Anus **2**:98, **3**:47, **7**:35
Anuscope **4**:87
Anxiety **1**:61–63, **5**:99
Aorta **1**:70, **6**:79
  coarctation of **2**:103
  overriding of **2**:103
  transposition of great vessels **2**:103–4
Aortic aneurysm **1**:47–49
Aortic stenosis **2**:102–3, **4**:69
Aortic valve **2**:102–3
Aphasia **1**:63–64
Aphthous ulcer **2**:38
Aplastic anemia **1**:44–45
Aplastic crisis **7**:87
Apnea **2**:62
  See also Sleep apnea
Apocrine glands **3**:105
Apoplexy. *See* Stroke
Appendicitis **1**:64–66, **3**:48, **8**:23
Appendicular skeleton **7**:96–97

Our thanks to the following organizations and persons who made the photographs used in this set possible:

Christ Episcopal Church Youth Program (Mary Millan)
Mount Vernon Teen Task Force (Chris Webb)
Putnam Family Support and Advocacy, Inc. (Pam Forde)

Photography assistant: Tania Gandy-Collins

MODELS
Roland Benson, Sally Bunch, Deirdre Burke, Kevin Chapin, Michael Clarke, Michelle Collins, Bryan Duggan, Germaine Elvy, Caitlin Faughnan, Imgard Kallenbach, Max Lipson, Lydia McCarthy, Amanda Moradel, Joshua Moradel, Veronica Moradel, Kate Peckham, Sara Pettinger, Mario Salinas, Heather Scogna, Halima Simmons, Wendy Sinclair, T.J. Trancynger, Rolando Walker, Deborah Whelan, Gregory Whelan, Francis Wick, Elaine Young, Leanne Young